THE CASTLE

SCENES FROM AN EXECUTION

By the same author

Stage Plays

> *Cheek*
> *No One Was Saved*
> *Alpha Alpha*
> *Edward, The Final Days*
> *Stripwell*
> *Claw*
> *The Love of a Good Man*
> *Fair Slaughter*
> *That Good Between Us*
> *The Hang of the Gaol*
> *The Loud Boy's Life*
> *Birth on a Hard Shoulder*
> *Crimes in Hot Countries*
> *No End of Blame*
> *Victory*
> *The Power of the Dog*
> *A Passion in Six Days*
> *Downchild*

TV Plays

> *Cows*
> *Mutinies*
> *Prowling Offensive*
> *Conrod*
> *Heroes of Labour*
> *Russia*
> *Credentials of a Sympathizer*
> *All Bleeding*
> *Heaven*
> *Pity in History*

Radio Plays

> *One Afternoon on the 63rd Level of the North Face*
>   *of the Pyramid of Cheops the Great*
> *Henry V in Two Parts*
> *Herman with Millie and Mick*
> *Scenes from an Execution*

Poetry

> *Don't Exaggerate; Desire and Abuse*

PLAYSCRIPT 110

THE CASTLE

SCENES FROM AN EXECUTION

Howard Barker

JOHN CALDER : LONDON
RIVERRUN PRESS : NEW YORK

First published in Great Britain, 1985, by
John Calder (Publishers) Limited
18 Brewer Street, London W1R 4AS

and in the United States of America, 1985, by
Riverrun Press Inc
1170 Broadway, New York, NY 10001

All performing rights in these plays are strictly reserved
and application for performance should be made to:

Judy Daish Associates Limited
83 Eastbourne Mews, London W6 6LQ

No performance of these plays may be given unless a licence
has been obtained prior to rehearsal.

British Library Cataloguing in Publication Data

Barker, Howard
 The castle : a triumph; Scenes from an
 execution.—(Playscript; no. 110)
 I. Title   II. Barker, Howard. Scenes from an
 execution
 822'.914   PR6052.A6485

ISBN 0-7145-4074-9

Typeset 9/10 pt Press Roman by Gilbert Composing Services,
Leighton Buzzard, Bedfordshire.
Printed in Great Britain by Hillman Printers (Frome), Somerset

For
Marcia Pointon

What is Politics, but the absence
of Desire . . . ?

THE CASTLE

A Triumph

CHARACTERS

STUCLEY	A Knight
BATTER	A Servant
KRAK	An Engineer
SKINNER	A Witch
ANN	A Changed Woman
NAILER	A Priest
CANT	A Villager
HUSH	A Villager
SPONGE	A Villager
HOLIDAY	A Builder
BRIAN	A Builder's Mate
POOL	A Circuit Judge
SOLDIERS	
PRISONERS	
WOMEN	

ACT ONE

Scene One

A Hill. A MAN, wrapped against the rain, stares into a valley. A SECOND MAN enters. He stares at the first.

BATTER. Thinking, this is a puddle, this is. This is a wet and bone-wrecking corner of Almighty negligence. Thinking, oh, these shifting sheets of dropping damp. Christ, I did wrong to, or Mohammed, is it? Oh, my sun, my date trees, you poor bugger, out of hot bricked yards and cool mosaics, YOU HAVE TO BE A GREAT HAIRY ENGLISH BASTARD TO WEAR THIS! OI! *(He tears open his clothing, exposing his chest to the weather)* England, your great frozen paw, OI! *(The other has not moved)* You are looking on my meadow. On my meadow which—*(He stares in disbelief)* NO CUNT HAS MOWN! *(He turns to ANOTHER off)* Have you seen this!

STUCLEY *enters, follows the direction of his finger.*

STUCLEY. Oh, the faithless bastards . . .
BATTER. Fallow, every fucking thing!
STUCLEY. Oh, the disloyal bastards . . .
BATTER. Not one in cultivation!
STUCLEY. My first glimpse and—
BATTER. And the wood not coppiced!
STUCLEY. My first glimpse and—
BATTER. And the pond not cleared, and no bugger with the cattle!
STUCLEY. ALL BASTARD ROTTEN! *(He turns to BATTER)* Ask them what they—my territory—what they—
BATTER *(running off)*. Hey!
STUCLEY. They have stripped me of every kind thought by this. Lying in their mess and squirming in the hot straw I imagine, while we suffered, I APOLOGIZE I FEEL SO ASHAMED! *(He shakes his head in despair)* All the good things I told you of this place and we clap eyes on the dead opposite. I'm glad it's raining, good! Piss rain you bastard sky, all I ever said is contradicted, good! All the glowing eyes round camp fires is pure fuck now, I'm lord of pigshit and made a proper fool of . . .
BATTER *(running, shouting)*. IT'S US! STUCLEY AND RETAINERS AFTER SEVEN YEARS!
STUCLEY. You stick yourself in every sordid place, and run your ribs against the stakes, chucking blood down by the panful, and what do they

3

do? They roost! They roost and shit the good estate in your absence, Christ, we will break their hearts for this! What are you staring at?

KRAK. I am looking at this hill, which is an arc of pure limestone . . .

STUCLEY. So it is, it is, yes, oh, I am so full of good, why does everything betray me? BECAUSE IT IS THE WAY OF THE WORLD! GOOD! All tenderness is doomed to ridicule, poetry is lies and mercy only fit for giggling over! IS MY WIFE DEAD? Must be, must be because I love her so, she's dead, it stands to reason, WHERE IS SHE BURIED? What was it, fever? Fever, merciful fever? No, she was banged to death by bandits, CAN YOU FIND SOMEONE OR NOT?

BATTER. Some filth is coming, I don't know who, some staggering filth, but I wouldn't know my mother after this time, if Christ had gilded her (*A* WOMAN *enters*). Do you know us or not?

CANT. You're Batter.

BATTER. She knows me! And my face ploughed up with scars!

CANT. Done much murder?

STUCLEY. DONE MUCH MURDER? DONE MUCH MURDER? I'M YOUR LORD YOU WHITE RAG, YOU!

CANT. How beautiful you are, you great male things, I would kiss you if you'd let me, or in the bush there something better—

STUCLEY. WHAT!

CANT. Oh, come on, we've had old men here, who only move by memory, not great stallion bits like yours, all—

STUCLEY. WHAT IS THIS!

CANT. My man's not come back so you do his business for him—here— *(She goes to lift her skirts. STUCLEY knocks her aside with a staggering blow)*

STUCLEY. I won't be fouled by you, mad bitch, what's happened here, what! I slash your artery for you! *(He draws a knife)* Down you, in the muck and nettle! *(She screams)* MY TERRITORY! *(He straddles her)*

BATTER. HEY! (STUCLEY *wounds her, she screams*)

STUCLEY. My shame, you—LOOK WHAT YOU'VE MADE ME DO! I've—I've *(He tosses the knife away, wipes his hand)* To come home and hear vile stuff of that sort is—when I am so clean for my lover is—no homecoming, is it?

KRAR. So much emotion, I think, is perfectly comprehensible, given the exertion of travelling, and all your exaggerated hopes. Some anticlimax is only to be expected.

STUCLEY. Yes. *(He shrugs)* Yes.

KRAK. The only requirement is the restoration of a little order, the rudiments of organization established, and so on. The garden is a little overgrown, and minds gone wild through lack of discipline. Chaos is only apparent in my experience, like gravel shaken in water abhors the turbulence, and soon asserts itself in perfect order. As for the absence of hospitality, that does not offend me either, but I should like a desk at some stage. *(Pause.* BATTER *stares at him)*

BATTER. Well, I'll be fucked *(Pause)* No, I will be. He raddles my brains, he does. He pits his long, dark fingers in my ears and stirs them up. GIVE

ME MY BRAINS BACK, YOU! *(He laughs, prods* CANT *with his boot)*
Get up. Buzz down the valley and tell the oh-so-honest English Stucley's
back with one mad retainer and a wog who can drawn perfect circles with
shut eyes. Run! *(He chases her off)*

STUCLEY. Wait! *(He looks to* KRAK*)* I run to my wife's bedroom. Catch
her unprepared and all confusion. Oh, my lord, etcetera, half her plaits
undone! Oh, my lord and all— *(He chases off)* Wait!

Pause. KRAK *is about to follow, when* A WOMAN *appears.*

ANN. My belly's a fist. Went clench on seeing you, went rock. And womb a
tumour. All my soft, rigid. What are you doing on my hill?

KRAK *(turning).* Looking. In so far as the mist permits.

ANN. It always rains like this for strangers. Drapes itself in a fine drench,
not liking to be spied on. A woman, this country, not arid like your place.
Not brazen. Were you captured and brought home to carry trays? *(He
looks at her)* My husband has turned skinny and beautiful. Was a fat
puppy when he left. Why was he not slaughtered like the others? Stood
around him, did they, taking arrows meant for him? The sole survivor of
some mincing scrap? NO ONE REQUIRES YOU BACK, TELL HIM.
*(*KRAK *bows)*

KRAK. You are the lady of this place, perhaps I might introduce—

ANN. No. Manners are vile and servants worse. Get off my hill. *(He starts
to go)* THIS WAS AN ORDINARY AFTERNOON AND NOW
YOU'RE HERE! *(He goes. A* SECOND WOMAN *enters)*

SKINNER. Stab him!

ANN. What—

SKINNER. Now! Stab him!

ANN. What—

SKINNER. I will!

ANN. Wait!

SKINNER. Wait, why wait!

ANN. You can't—we haven't—WE HAVEN'T DISCUSSED THIS—

SKINNER. Fuck, he's running!

ANN. Catch him, then—

SKINNER. Can't, can't now, hey! Come and be stabbed! *(Pause)* He's
gone into a thicket. *(Pause)*

ANN. I hope that wasn't—I do hope that wasn't—THE MOMENT
AFTER WHICH—the fulcrum of disaster—I hope not.

SKINNER. Miss one moment, twice as hard next time. Miss the next time,
ten times as hard the next.

ANN. All right—

SKINNER. Block the trickle before it's a stream, block the stream before
it's a river—

ANN. ALL RIGHT, I SAID. Kill him later. What is he, anyway, a quaint
slave to cook weird Turkish afters. The damp will do him if we don't.

SKINNER. You called him beautiful. Your husband. Beautiful, you said.

ANN. He was. The bone has made an appearance. *(Pause)* Well, he is. HE
IS.

SKINNER. You won't—

ANN. I called him beautiful, I saw his face and it—

SKINNER. Go all cream and butter for his paddle, tell me—

ANN. Simple description of his face—

SKINNER. I WON'T ALLOW IT. *(Pause)*

ANN. You go so ugly, in a second, at the bid of a thought, so ugly.

SKINNER. I love you, that's what makes me ugly.

ANN. And your eyes shrink to points, and your mouth collapses . . . *(They embrace. CANT enters)*

CANT. Bugger cut me with a dagger, look! *(She exposes a breast)*

ANN. Where are they?

CANT. In the big 'ouse, going barmy. Stucley's chucked the loom out, picked it up and dropped it in the shit 'eap. Batter's slicin' old men 'ho used to carry 'im round on their backs. Lovely. 'e works the point under their skin an' twists it. They wanna know 'ho made all the babies.

ANN. Nobody told them?

CANT. Too fuckin' true, nobody told 'em. So Stucley goes to the church for consolation and finds it locked an' pigeons shittin' up the belfry. 'e goes screamin' mad and puts 'is foot through all the winders. Only the wog stays still, kneels in the parlour cooking something 'e calls coffee. Look, my tit's bleedin'!

ANN. Tell him I'm here. On the hill, tell him.

CANT. Why ain't she 'ere, 'e says, plaited and fragrant? Plaited an' fragrant! Bugger!

ANN. Tell him. He'll come.

CANT. I'll see what mood 'e's in. An' fuck you if 'e's wavin' daggers, I won't say nothin'. *(She goes to leave, stops)* Are they stayin'? *(Pause)* I'm only askin'. If they're stayin'? *(Pause, she goes out)*

SKINNER. First there was the bailiff, and we broke the bailiff. And then there was God, and we broke God. And lastly there was cock, and we broke that, too. Freed the ground, freed religion, freed the body. And went up this hill, standing together naked like the old female pack, growing to eat and not to market, friends to cattle who we milked but never slaughtered, joining the strips and dancing in the commons, the three days' labour that we gave to priests gave instead to the hungry, turned the tithe barn into a hospital and FOUND CUNT BEAUTIFUL that we had hidden and suffered shame for, its lovely shapelessness, its colour all miraculous, what they had made dirty or worshipped out of ignorance, do we now—

ANN. No—

SKINNER. Just deliver it—

ANN. No—

SKINNER. Our bodies and our labour up to their groping fingers?

ANN. No. *(Pause)*

SKINNER. I helped your births. And your conceptions. Sat by the bedroom, at the door, while you took the man's thing in you, shuddering with disgust and trying hard to see it only as the mating of dumb cattle—

ANN. It was—

SKINNER. Yes, and I managed. I did manage. And washed you, and parted your hair. I never knew such intimacy, did you? Tell me, all this unity!

ANN. Never—

SKINNER. And my husband's bones are kicked around the hills of Asia. Husband. The suffocating thing in darkness. Oh, good for wars in foreign places, let them stab away for Christ or Mohammed! And I prayed to everything not one of them would crawl back to this valley, but I was not a good enough witch, was I?

ANN. No . . .

SKINNER. They crossed the world, missed floods and avalanches—

ANN. Loose planks on bridges—

SKINNER. Snake bites—

ANN. Falling trees and plague villages—

SKINNER. Angry parents of raped daughters—

ANN. Barmy tribesmen—

SKINNER. And rancid whores whose cunts dripped instant death, how did they? Europe is a million miles long, isn't it, how did they pick their way back here, AN ANT COULD PASS THROUGH A BONFIRE EASIER! (ANN *laughs.* SKINNER *looks at her)* How? *(Pause)*

ANN. Why are you looking at me like that?

SKINNER. How, then?

ANN. I suppose because—

SKINNER. You drew him. *(Pause)*

ANN. What?

SKINNER. Drew him. With your underneath. *(Pause)*

ANN. I do think—if we—

SKINNER. DOWN THERE CALLED TO HIM ACROSS THE SPACES!

ANN. Look—

SKINNER. I HATE GOD AND NATURE, THEY MADE US VIOLABLE AS BITCHES!

ANN *clasps her, sobbing with anger.* STUCLEY *enters, holding a white garment. Pause.*

STUCLEY. Put this on, please. *(They look at him)* I found it in the bottom of a trunk. Do wear it, please. Change in the bushes, as you like this place so much. *(He looks at* SKINNER) And you, Skinner's widow, clear off.

SKINNER. Don't be the wife to him, don't—

STUCLEY. GET OUT.

ANN *(To* SKINNER). Go on Trust me. Go on. (SKINNER *withdraws.* STUCLEY *still holds out the garment)*

STUCLEY. Trust you? Why? *(He looks at her)* You look so—*(Pause)* Trust you? Why? *(Pause)* Imagine what I—if you would condescend to—what I—the riot of my feelings when I look at—*(Pause)* Trust you to do what exactly? *(Pause)* In seven years I have aged twenty. And you, if anything, have grown younger, so we who were never boy and girl exactly have now met in some middling maturity, I have seen your face on tent roofs, don't laugh at me, will you? *(Pause)*

ANN. No.

STUCLEY. That is a ploughman's hag and you—what is it, exactly? *(Pause)* I found the church bunged up with cow and bird dung, the place we married in, really, what—*(Pause)* So I prayed in the nettles. *(Pause)* Very devout picture of young English warrior returning to his domain etcetera get your needle out and make a tapestry why don't you? Or don't you do that any more? *(Pause)* Christ knows what goes on here, you must explain to me over the hot milk at bedtime, everything changes and dreams are bollocks but you can't help dreaming, even knowing a dream is—*(Pause)* It is quite amusing coming back to this I was saying to the Arab every hundred yards I have this little paradise and he went mmm and mmm he knew the sardonic bastard, they are not romantic like us are they, muslims, and they're right! Please put this on because I—

ANN. No. *(Pause)*

STUCLEY. This wedding thing, you were sixteen years my senior and a widow and I trembled, didn't I, and you said, do not feel you must do anything, but may I kiss you I have always loved your mouth WHY WON'T YOU PUT IT ON. *(Pause)* So there we were thinking—it is not a desert, actually, it is full of fields and orchards the Holy Land—and some said tell my old lady I was killed and married Arab women or Jewesses, some of them. Fewer were killed than you might think, much fewer, after all we left with fifty and it was tempting, obviously, but I thought she—wrongly it appears—she— *(Pause)* Have children in two continents, most of them. Not me, though. Not in one, alas. *(Pause)* I thought the time had come to—it was meant to be two years, not seven, but you know—or perhaps you don't—how wars go—coming back was worse than anything—what we did in Hungary I would not horrify you with—they got more barmy by the hour. Not me, though. I thought she'll take my bleeding feet in her warm place, she'll lay me down in clean sheets and work warm oils into my skin and food, we'll spend whole days at—but everything is contrary, must be, mustn't it, I who jumped in every pond of murder kept this one thing pure in my head, pictured you half-naked on an English night, your skin which was translucent from one angle and deep-furrowed from another, your odour even which I caught once in the middle of a scrap, do you believe that, even smells are stored, I'm sorry I chucked your loom out of the window, amazing strength comes out of temper, it's half a ton that thing if it's—trust me, what does that mean?

ANN. You've not changed. Thinner, but the same. For all the marching and the stabbing. Whereas quietly, here I have.

STUCLEY *(tossing the garment aside)*. Fuck the garment! Get to bed with me and we'll stir up long forgotten feelings, go down deep to floors of fornication we've not—

ANN. It isn't possible—

STUCLEY. IT IS, YOU LIE DOWN AND YOU PART YOURSELF. *(Pause)* They say coarse things, by habit almost. Not me, though, I tried to keep my language wholesome and—not difficult if you have faith—

ANN. You shouldn't have—

STUCLEY. I shouldn't have? What? What shouldn't I?

ANN. Have struggled to be pure.

STUCLEY. No struggle! If you have faith!

ANN. Have kept the perfect husband for me—

STUCLEY. WHY NOT, BECAUSE YOU WERE NOT EQUAL? *(Pause)*

ANN. No. *(Pause. He is suspended between hysteria and disbelief)*

STUCLEY. I think when God says—CRUSH THIS BASTARD—I wish there was a priest here, but there isn't so I offer you my version, you hark to my theology—he really is the most THOROUGHGOING OF ALL DEITIES, no wonder we all bow down to him his grasp of pain and pressure is so exquisite and all comprehending, what human torturer, what miserable nail-wrenching amateur in pain could pit his malevolence against the celestial wit and come out on top, no man I assure you could conceive of so many alleys by which to turn a brain. As if I had not swallowed every vileness conceivable and still stand on two feet, He chooses to hamstring me not by your death—that I had always reckoned possible, that I expected hourly to be splashed in my face, but no, he has me from her own mouth hear my lady has acquiesced in the riot of her cunt! And I have just fought the Holy War on His behalf! Oh, Lord and Master of Cruelty, who has no shred of mercy for thy servants, I worship Thee! *(He kneels, lowering his head to the ground)* There is no arguing with genius like this, I threw the dagger away, it's in the bushes somewhere or I might have slit you open, but He takes care of everything, He does, oh, praise Thee, praise Thee, now tell me she has children by the very interlopers who greeted me as I climbed my very own steps.

ANN. Yes.

STUCLEY. Yes! Yes! I know the source of our religion! It is that He in His savagery is both excessive and remorseless and to our shrieks both deaf and blind! I could be a bishop. I missed my chance, slicing black men on the banks of the Jordan, silly, that's for sloggers and boys obsessed with weapons, no, the bishops have got their tongues in God's arse and lick up the absolute, that's for me, PASS A BIT OF PURPLE SOMEBODY! How many bastards, then?

ANN. One and three died.

STUCLEY. And you past forty! Such fertility, the Lord denying even his own ordinances to make me squirm, she will be pupping in her dotage if it hurts me, and I spent enough juice in you to father forty regiments and not one bred, further evidence, if evidence you needed of His mighty genius, bow, bow, Thou who dost not miss a trick! *(He bumps his head on the ground)* Bow, bow . . . *(He stops, laughing)* Could be furious. Not me, though. *(He gets up)* I met somebody who put a lock on it. His lady's thing. Had locked it! Really, the barbarism! And got a lance through him at Acre and fell into the sea, and sank, down to the floor of the blue waters, man and single key. Well, you couldn't have two keys, could you! *(He laughs)* You have to laugh, I do, I have great recourse to laughter, of the demonic variety, I could kill you and no one would bat an eyelid. *(Pause)*

ANN. Don't stay.

STUCLEY. Don't stay?

ANN. No. Be welcome, and pass through.

STUCLEY.   One night and then—
ANN.   Yes.
STUCLEY.   What—in the stable, kip down and—
ANN.   Not in the stable.
STUCLEY.   Not in the stable? You mean I might—
ANN.   Don't, please, become sarcastic, it—
STUCLEY.   Inside the house, perhaps, we might just—
ANN.   Useless sarcasm, it—
STUCLEY.   Under the stairs, and creep away at first light—
ANN.   Undermines your honour—
STUCLEY.   WHAT HONOUR YOU DISHEVELLED AND IMPER-
TINENT SLAG. *(Pause)* You see, you make me lose my temper, you make
me abusive, why not stay, it is my home.
ANN.   Not now.
STUCLEY.   Not now, why not?
ANN.   There have been changes.
STUCLEY.   I begin to see, but where do you propose we—
ANN.   Go on.
STUCLEY.   To where?
ANN.   The horizon.
STUCLEY.   I own the horizon.
ANN.   Cross it, then. *(Pause)* I'm cruel, but I do it to be simple. To cut off
hopes cleanly. No tearing wounds, I'm sorry if your dreams are spoiled
but—
STUCLEY.   It is perfectly kind of you—
ANN.   Not kind—
STUCLEY.   Yes, perfectly kind and typically considerate of you, I do
appreciate the instinct but—
ANN.   Not kind, I say—
STUCLEY.   YES! Down on your knees, now.
ANN.   What—
STUCLEY.   On your knees, now—
ANN.   Are you going to be—
STUCLEY.   Down, now—
ANN.   Childish and—
STUCLEY.   Yes, I WAS YOUR CHILD, WASN'T I? *(Pause. He suddenly
weeps. She watches him, then goes to him. He embraces her, then thrusts her
away)* PENITENCE FOR ADULTERY! *(He sees a figure off, calls)* HOI!
Tell me what's gone on, they've abolished the apology! *(An OLD MAN
enters)* They do their sin with such clear eyes! Are you a thief, or been up in
my bedroom? The more innocent you look, the more sunk in treachery, it
stands to reason! Do you know me?
HUSH.   Yes—
STUCLEY.   Oh, good, I'm known, GET DOWN THEN! It is going to
take—this restoration of authority—a lot of time and bruising, I can see!
ANN.   Don't make him bend.
STUCLEY.   Why not, old bugger!
ANN.   We've done with bending here.

STUCLEY *(forcing him to the ground)*. Done with it? It's nature!

HUSH.   Forgive me, forgive me!

STUCLEY.   Forgive, what for?

HUSH.   Whatever offends you—

STUCLEY.   Good! Oh, good! The first wise words since I set foot in my domain! He is not grey for nothing, he has scuttled through his eighty years with sorry on his lips, spewed sorry out for each and every occasion, good! I appreciate you, cunning licker of brute crevices, insinuator of beds and confidences. Kiss my hands and tell me what you did against me. The more extravagant, the more credence I attach to it, promise you.

HUSH.   I did not praise you in your absence.

STUCLEY.   Oh, that's nothing, you mean you abused me, surely?

HUSH   Abused you, yes.

STUCLEY.   Excellent, go on.

ANN.   This is disgusting.

STUCLEY.   Disgusting? No, he longs for his confession!

HUSH.   I did not tend your meadows or your stock—

STUCLEY.   You mean you stole them off me?

HUSH.   Stole them, yes. I did not pray for your safe return—

STUCLEY.   Oh, shit this for a confession, this is the Valley of wickedness, say you prayed for my slow-dying torture—

HUSH.   Yes!

STUCLEY.   Daily prayed the devil I would rot—

HUSH.   Yes!

STUCLEY.   Turned my house into a brothel, my bedroom, whooped in it—

HUSH.   Yes—

STUCLEY.   Go on, I am confessing for you, you do it!

HUSH.   Adultery and fornication—

STUCLEY.   On who? On her?

HUSH.   On everyone!

ANN.   I won't witness this—

STUCLEY *(grabbing her wrist)*. Must witness it! *(To* HUSH*)* Stuck children on her, did you?

HUSH.   Yes!

STUCLEY.   No, in your words!

HUSH.   I lay on her and others naked and did put my seed in them and—

STUCLEY.   Oh, rubbish, it's beyond belief. I hate bad lies, lies that fall apart, there's no entertainment in them. Get on your cracking pins, you tottering old bugger . . . (ANN *helps* HUSH *to his feet*)

HUSH.   Thank you.

STUCLEY.   Thank me, why?

HUSH.   Because the worst thing in age is the respect. The smile of condescension, and the hush with which the most banal opinion is received. The old know nothing. Fling them down. They made the world and they need punishing.

STUCLEY.   Good, I've no regrets if half your bones are out of joint.

HUSH.   Me neither.

STUCLEY.   I cherish nothing, cherishing's out, and what was soft in me
has liquified into a poison puddle. Not to be fooled. That's my dream now,
THANK YOU, UNIVERSE! *(Pause)* Educated me. Educated me . . . *(He
goes out)*

ANN.   Tell him nothing.

HUSH.   I won't.

ANN.   Not even thank you or good morning.

HUSH.   No.

ANN.   He'll kill you if he knows you fathered children on me. Some vile
Turkish torture. Do you want that?

HUSH.   No.

ANN.   Good. Half the children in this valley are off you.

HUSH.   As many as that?

ANN.   Yes, so keep your mouth shut.

HUSH.   Promise you. *(He starts to go out)*

ANN.   Why do you love your life so much? *(He stops)* So much that even
dignity gets spewed, and truth kicked into blubber, and will itself as pliable
as a string of gut? You have no appetite but life itself, I mean breathing and
continuing. *(He shrugs)* There can't be a man alive with more children and
less interest in the world they grow up in.

HUSH.   I never sought my family . . .

ANN.   No. You were led to the female and then turned back in the field
again . . . *(He turns to go)* IF YOU ACHIEVE IMMORTALITY I SHALL
BE FURIOUS.

Scene Two

Another day. BATTER *carries a desk on his back. He is followed by an* OLD
MAN *carrying paraphernalia.*

BATTER.   Down here, you quivering old bum, you walnut bollock,
and careful with the precious instruments! *(He lowers the tools)* This is
the impediment of science, which in collusion with his genius will wring
transformation out the dozing landscape. And he is mine, in all his
rareness, mine, as if I'd birthed him, yes, DON'T LOOK AT ME LIKE
THAT, I am his second mother! Through me, brute flesh and knuckle,
he has existence, who might be just another husk of wogland, sons of
Arabia blowing in the sand, I saved him, I, who was running head to
foot with Arab gore, kicked back the door and saw him, and he stared
into my eye, my eyes which were—THE ONLY BLUE—the rest being
hot gore, and into my only blues his only browns stared pleadingly . . .
imagine it . . .

SPONGE.   I can . . .

BATTER.   You can . . . you can imagine nothing . . . This was the middle of
Jerusalem where every bastard male or female I trod by was split and
opened up to inquisitive old daylight. I SPARED NO ONE. Well, we had

been outside in rain and snow for seven months, there is snow in deserts . . .

SPONGE.   I can imagine . . .

BATTER.   No one who was not there can imagine anything. Never say 'I can imagine' again. It's a lie, nobody can. And he stared into the little lights of what must have been—my kindness—and I stopped, the dagger in my hand tipped this way . . . and that . . . slippery in my fist. I pondered. AFTER EIGHTEEN STAIRCASES OF MURDER . . . and of course, because I pondered, the genius was safe. Funny. Funny that I pondered when this was the very bugger who designed the fort; the |pen| was |in| his fingers for some lethal innovation. HOW MANY MORE DEAD WOULD THAT HAVE COST?

SPONGE.   I can't imagine . . .

BATTER.   Not that I care about death, not even my own. In little avenues and parks they fret on death who have so rigorously hid from life— (KRAK *comes in*) Have you done murder, genius? *(He goes to him, holds his hands)* Not with those hands, no, but that is SHIT HYPOCRISY— (KRAK *withdraws from him*) It is, because the line from a to b—you see, I have education, too—the linear trapezoid para—fucking—llelogram is FIVE HUNDRED CORPSES LONG! No offence to mathematics, no offence.

Cries off. STUCLEY *enters dragging a* MAN *by the neck.*

STUCLEY.   Found him! Found him! My incumbent priest who did the wedlock whilst squirming at his celibacy! True or false?

NAILER *(his neck wrenched).* True!

STUCLEY.   The knob beneath the vestment twirling at my vows! It's all here, everything we left is like old ruins underneath the grass! Are we making too much noise? I know you have to concentrate. (KRAK *is leaning on the desk, staring across the valley*) This man married me, and when I was away, condoned my bitch's filth! I do believe, I do believe this, that human beings left without severity would roll back the ages and be hopping, croaking frogs, clustering thick on the female with the coming of the Spring, and sunk in mud for winter . . . !

KRAK.   The castle is not a house. *(They look at him)* The castle is not a house.

NAILER.   No lord's land, we said, and no common land, we said, but every man who lives shall go as he pleases, and we threw the fences down and made a bad word of fence, we called fence blasphemy, the only word we deemed so, all the rest we freed, the words for women's and men's parts we liberated—

BATTER *(To* KRAK). Come again?

NAILER.   And freeing the words we also freed the—

BATTER.   Not you. (NAILER *stops. Pause*)

STUCLEY.   What is the castle, then? (KRAK *does not respond.* STUCLEY *turns to* BATTER) Lock this in God's house and make him wash it spotless and set up God's furniture again.

NAILER *(pulled out).* God has no furniture.

STUCLEY.   No, but the church has! (NAILER *and* BATTER *go out*) I tell you, the world's here as we left it, just sunk a bit, like the Roman pavement; you scuff it up, you spit, and there's the sun shining out the mosaic, an old god never properly obscured, Mithras waiting for his hour. So with vicars who have gone barmy, there is the old tithe gatherer beneath some weed of fancy patter I bet you . . . *(Pause)* Go on . . . (KRAK *holds out a large paper*) Has he made a drawing for me? *(He smiles)* He has . . . *(He looks at* KRAK, *beaming)* The Great Amazer! *(He takes it, looks at it)* Which way up is it? *(He turns it round and round)* I genuflect before the hieroglyphs but what—

KRAK.   No place is not watched by another place. (STUCLEY *nods*) The heights are actually depths.

STUCLEY.   Yup.

KRAK.   The weak points are actually strong points.

STUCLEY.   Yup.

KRAK.   The entrances are exits.

STUCLEY.   Yes!

KRAK.   The doors lead into pits.

STUCLEY.   Go on!

KRAK.   It resembles a defence but is really an attack.

STUCLEY.   Yes—

KRAK.   It cannot be destroyed—

STUCLEY.   Mmm—

KRAK.   Therefore it is a threat—

STUCLEY.   Mmm—

KRAK.   It will make enemies where there are none—

STUCLEY.   You're losing me—

KRAK.   It makes war necessary—(STUCLEY *looks at him*) It is the best thing I have ever done.

STUCLEY's *long stare is interrupted by a racket of construction as a massive framework for a spandrel descends slowly to the floor. On the construction,* BUILDERS *and the master,* HOLIDAY. STUCLEY *goes out.*

HOLIDAY.   Oh, Christ, Oh, bleeding hell, somebody!

WORKMAN *(calling to someone above)*. Steady, Brian!

HOLIDAY.   I never should, I never should, should I? Expose myself to—are we safe? Are we down yet?

WORKMAN.   Cast off, Brian!

HOLIDAY *(whose eyes are shut)*. I am in the wrong trade, can I open my eyes, are we—

WORKMAN.   Down, Harry!

HOLIDAY.   Down, are we? *(He opens his eyes)* Oh, lovely earth, immobile, stationary thing! *(He kisses it)* Do you sympathize with my condition? I exaggerate of course, I exaggerate to win the pity of my workmen. It is a good thing to advertize your weakness, it obliges them to demonstrate their manliness. Are you afraid of heights? When I am up I am horrified in case I slip between the boards, and when I'm down afraid some hammer will be dropped and plop through my cranium. I have an eggshell skull and yet I am a builder, that is one of life's perversities. In thirty years I have built two castles and an abbey and this tilt to my head is permanent, I have one eye always on the sky which may at any moment hold my extinction in some falling implement, what is wrong with the women found here, I am actually fond of women, when I did the abbey had some decent conversation with the nuns but this—

Enter SKINNER, *draped in flowers.*

SKINNER. OLD HILL SAYS NO.

HOLIDAY. Does it, never 'eard it—

SKINNER. ROCK WEEPS AND STONE PROTESTS—

HOLIDAY. *(calling off)*. Brian, I will 'ave that templet for the blind arch when you're ready—

SKINNER. *(turning to* KRAK). Weren't you loved? Some bit of you not nourished? Why are all your things hard things, compasses, nibs and protractors, the little armoury of your drawing board, have you looked at a flower, go on, take one, the superior geometry of the— *(He ignores her)* WHY DON'T YOU LOOK AT A FLOWER!

HOLIDAY. *(shouting up)*. No, I won't come up there, I 'ave just been up there—

SKINNER. *(turning back to* HOLIDAY*)*. The flower—five petals—each petal identical—LOOK AT THE FLOWER, WILL YOU, IT'S GOT TRUTH IN IT—all right, don't look at it, why should I save you, why should I educate you—

HOLIDAY. *(still addressing his foreman)*. All right, do it your way—

SKINNER. Educate you, oh yes, educate him, look at him—

HOLIDAY. I said—

SKINNER. My breath, my knowledge, really, do you believe I'd—what—on this—

HOLIDAY. I said do it—

SKINNER. Waste my precious—on you—all my struggle through the dark, through clinging—really, on you—does he actually—

HOLIDAY. I'M SORRY, BRIAN, 'OW CAN I FUCKING CONCEN-TRATE!

SKINNER. SAVE YOU, YOU ARE NOT FIT! *(Pause. He looks at her)* No, no, no time for it. Educate you and they pile up bricks, love to educate you but—oh, love to, but—look, the footings in already, go back where you came from, quick, this will not be finished, you coat is on the hook, run without stopping even though it hurts your hanging guts, run, I tell you, I know, I am the witch, quick. *(Pause. He stares at her)* Quick . . .

BATTER *comes in, looks at her. She turns her head to him contemptuously, then flings up her skirts and shows her arse. She walks off.*

BATTER. Supposed to be a woman. A woman, calls itself.

HOLIDAY. Never saw a nun do that—

BATTER. No, well, you wouldn't—

HOLIDAY. Not in all the—

BATTER. A nun wouldn't, would she? Not a normal nun—

HOLIDAY. Barmy—

BATTER. Barmy, yes—

HOLIDAY. They 'ad their moods, they 'ad their comings-over as all women do, but—are these towers really going to be ninety foot above the curtain? I don't complain, every slab is food and drink to me, but ninety foot? Who are you—it's a quiet country what I see of it—no, the woman's touched, surely?

BATTER. *(contemplatively)*. Skinner's arse . . .

HOLIDAY. What?

BATTER. He told me how he lay upon that arse, and she kept stiff as rock, neither moaning nor moving, but rock. So when the bishop asked for soldiers he was first forward, to get shot of her with Christ's permission. And found a girl under the olives, who moved with him and praised him. Well, he assumed so, they had not a word in common. And he kept on, the difference in women, the difference in women! But she outlasts him. There is no justice, is there? *(He turns to* KRAK) Is there? No justice?

BRIAN. *(entering)*. Michael wants you about the quoins.

HOLIDAY. I will see Michael—

BRIAN. The courses for the quoins, 'e says—

HOLIDAY. Thank you, Brian—

BRIAN. Don' tally with the specifications—

HOLIDAY. I will attend to Michael! I will explain to Michael 'ow many courses there are to the quoins—

BRIAN. Okay.

HOLIDAY. I will simplify the already simple drawing which his eyes are crossing over, but don't 'urry me! When you 'urry, you forget, and when you forget, that is the moment the dropped chisel is hastening to its rendezvous with the distracted 'ead. I will join Michael, but at my own bidding, thank you. *(*BRIAN *goes out)* This is all new to me. This passion for the circle. Leaving aside the embrasures and the lintels, there are no corners. Are none of the walls straight? Perpendicular, yes, but straight? (KRAK *ignores him)* Out of curiosity, what was wrong with square towers? *(Pause)* Just change, is it? Just novelty? *(Pause. He desists)* All right, I'm coming! *(He goes out.* BATTER *watches* KRAK)

KRAK. Dialogue is not a right, is it? When idiots waylay geniuses, where is the obligation? *(Pause)* And words, like buckets, slop with meanings. *(Pause)* To talk, what is that but the exchange of clumsy approximations, the false endeavour to share knowledge, the false endeavour to disseminate truths arrived at in seclusion? *(Pause)* When the majority are, perceptibly, incapable of the simplest intellectual discipline, what is the virtue of incessant speech? The whole of life serves to remind us we exist among inert banality. *(Pause)* I only state the obvious. The obvious being the starting point of architecture, as of any other science . . .

BATTER. Very good, but why so big? I don't think even Acre was this big, the citadel, was it? The walls of this you could accomodate the parish in, all to be paid for out of what, I wonder? You have your methods, I expect, but these bitches never cropped for surpluses, and kept the sheep for pets as far as I can see, the wool was hanging off the hedges, paid for out of what, I wonder? *(Pause)* And when they throw open the shutters, where's the sky, they'll say, give us back our fucking sky, they will, won't they? All they'll clap eyes on is masonry and arrow slits, it will blot the old blue out and throw long shadows over them, always at the corner of their eye, kissing or clawing, even in the bedroom looking in, and drunken arses falling out of beer houses will search in vain for corners to piss in not overlooked. Why? *(Pause)* Or don't you spend words on me, perhaps I'm only, what—inert banality? What's that, you bilingual fucker, you have more words in a foreign tongue than I have in English, but then I have the dagger, who speaks volumes when it comes to it, INERT BANALITY I christen it! *(He kisses the blade. Thunder and black)*

Scene Three

In semi-darkness, the figure of BRIAN *running from the building works. He is followed by* CANT, *pursued by* SKINNER. SKINNER *catches her.*

CANT. I DONE NOTHIN'!

SKINNER. You unravel us! What we knit together you unstitch!

CANT. I DONE NO WRONG, LET GO YOU!

SKINNER. I don't hurt you, do I? Don't struggle and I—you are asking to be—*(She brings* CANT *to the ground)* There, I do that because you—*(She sees her own clothes are muddied)* look at me—we slither in their mess— this was all bluebell once—patience, though, I am listening to you, I am all ears why you were in the foundations with a brickie—

CANT. Wasn't!

SKINNER. Oh, this is too painful for excuses!

CANT. Well, I wasn't—what you were thinking—wasn't anyway—

SKINNER. No—

CANT. DEFINITELY NOT!

SKINNER. But while we're on the subject . . . *(Pause)*

CANT. I haven't—you know I haven't—ever really overcome my—not ever conquered my weakness for—*(Pause)* It was easy before the builders come, but there are dozens of these geezers and they—I gaze at their trousers, honestly I do, whilst thinking, enemy, enemy! I do gaze so, though hating myself, obviously . . .

ANN. *(entering).* What?

SKINNER. In the footings with a brickie—

CANT. ONLY TO KEEP THE RAIN OFF!

SKINNER. What? Off what?

ANN. With her it is just—it is a hunger—I don't see what—

SKINNER. Punish her, of course!

ANN. When she is like she is? What—

SKINNER. Yes!

CANT. I DON'T WANNA BE PUNISHED!

SKINNER. You give her the truth, and she rejects the truth—

CANT. Skinner, I don't want to be—

SKINNER. And rejecting the truth she wrecks herself, and wrecking herself she wrecks others, and wrecking others—

CANT. Skinner—

SKINNER. *(turning on* CANT). They occupy your mind with that! WE MADE OURSELVES WHEN WE DITCHED THAT!

ANN. You are too angry—

SKINNER. Angry? Me? What? Mustn't be angry, no, be good, Skinner, be tolerant, her feelings being somewhat coarse what do you expect of peasant women, farmworkers ever on their backs, legs open in the crops, LISTEN, we all bring to the world, inside our skulls, inside our bellies, Christ knows what lumber from our makers BUT. You do not lie down to the burden, you toss it off. The whine 'I am made like that' will not wash, will it? Correct me if I'm wrong, will it? We have done such things here and they come back and straddle us, where is the strength if we go up against the walls skirts up and occupied like that? *(Pause)* I do think, I do think, to understand is not to condone, is it? *(Pause)* I do feel so alone, do you feel that? *(Pause)* It always rains here, which we loved once. I love you and I wish we could just love, but no, this is the test, all love is tested, or else it cannot know its power . . .

CANT. I'm sorry.

SKINNER. The words, the words go drip, drip, drip . . .

CANT. Said I'm sorry, didn't I! (ANN *indicates she should go.* CANT *slips away)*

SKINNER. Where there are builders, there are whores, and where there are whores, there are criminals, and after the criminals come the police, the great heap heaving, and what was peace and simple is dirt and struggle, and where there was a field to stand up straight in there is loud and frantic city. Stucley will make a city of this valley, what does he say to you?

ANN. Nothing.

SKINNER. No, nothing, and every day I expected to be stabbed or stifled, didn't you? What is this waiting for? You have been here ten minutes and not said you love me. I suspect you terribly without a shred of evidence, I shall spoil us with it. Is it because you were happy with him once? You see, I never was, never with a man, and you so fecund and me horribly childless—

ANN. Not horribly—

SKINNER. Not horribly, no—

ANN. I don't declare my feelings—

SKINNER. No, you don't—

ANN. Can't be forever declaring feelings, you declare yours, over and over, but—

SKINNER. Yes—

ANN. It is your way—

SKINNER. Ridiculous way—

ANN. I am not forthcoming with these statements you require, you have to trust—

SKINNER. Yes—

ANN. Signs, more. *(Pause)*

SKINNER. I do. I do trust signs. *(Pause)* We do not make a thing of flesh, do we, the love of women is more—they could eat flesh from off your body, we—no, actually I could eat yours, I could! Tell me why you love me!

ANN. I don't see that I need, do I, need to—

SKINNER. Oh, come on, yes, you do need to, and I will tell why I love you, the more they bore into the hill the more we must talk love, the bond, fasten it tighter! You are very cold this evening, I am not imagining it, you'll say I'm imagining it, but—

ANN. Yes. *(Pause)*

SKINNER. What, then. (ANN *does not reply)* They talk of a love-life, don't they? Do you know the phrase 'love-life', as if somehow this thing ran under or beside, as if you stepped from one life to the other, banality to love, love to banality, no, love is in the cooking and the washing and the milking, no matter what, the colour of the love stains everything, I say so anyway, being admittedly of a most peculiar disposition I WOULD RATHER YOU WERE DEAD THAN TOOK A STEP OR SHUFFLE BACK FROM ME. Dead, and I would do it. There I go, WHAT IS IT YOU LOOK SO DISTANT.

ANN. I think you are—obsessive. *(Pause)*

SKINNER. Obsessive, me? Obsessive? *(Pause. She fights down something)* I nearly got angry, then and nearly went—no—I will not—and—wait, the anger sinks—*(Pause)* Like tipping water on the sand, the anger goes, the anger vanishes— into what? I've no idea, my entrails, I assume. I do piss anger in the night, my pot is angerfull. *(Pause)* I am obsessive, why aren't you? *(Pause)* Every stone they raise is aimed at us. And things we have not dreamed of yet will come from it. Poems, love and gardening will be—and where you turn your eyes will be—and even the little middle of your heart which you think is your safe and actual self will be—transformed by it. I don't know how but even the way you plait your hair will be determined by it, and what we crop and even the colour of the babies, I do think it's odd, so odd, that when you resist you are obsessive but when you succumb you are not WHOSE OBSESSION IS THIS THING or did you mean my love, they are the same thing actually. *(Pause)* They have a corridor of dungeons and somewhere are the occupants, they do not know yet and she fucked in there, not knowing it, of course, not being a witch could not imagine far enough, it is the pain of witches to see to the very end of things . . .

ANN. Yes.

SKINNER. What?

ANN. To all you say and yet—I think I must talk with my husband. *(Pause)*

SKINNER. Talk—

ANN. Yes, he is not as you—

SKINNER. Your what?

ANN. He also has got feeling and—

SKINNER. Talk to your what—

ANN. I have a right to sense as well as you! *(Pause)* Even Nailer has recanted. Kneeling is back and they have not put the keep up yet.

SKINNER. There is no talking between you and a man. No talking. Words, yes, the patter and the eyes on your belt—

ANN. How shall we win!

SKINNER. I do not know how we will win! It is not a failing not to know the end at the beginning. Our power comes out of our love. Love also is a weapon. *(Pause)*

ANN. Yes. *(Pause)*

SKINNER. The way you say yes . . . *(Pause)* We lay under the stars, and in the comfort of the trees swaying, the felled trees, swaying, swore everlasting love. I will not accept that everlasting love, even as you swear it, is a lie, a permissible lie, because you do not know the unforeseen condition. It is still everlasting, there could be forty thousand murderers or forty thousand starving children, violence or pity threatening, it still takes precedence.—*(She turns swiftly)* Who is there, exactly? *(She addresses the shadows)* Are you interested in love? Give us your opinion. I am in the grip of this eccentric view that sworn love is binding—

KRAK *steps out of the shadows.*

KRAK. Why not? If sworn hatred is. *(They look at him. He goes to leave)*

ANN. I wonder if you smile? I have never seen you.

SKINNER. Don't talk to him. Accuse him.

ANN *(ignoring her)*. Or laugh, for that matter. But most laughter's false. I trust smiles better.

SKINNER. No, that's talking—

ANN. Have you no children? I somehow think you have not looked in children's eyes—

SKINNER. DO YOU THINK HE LISTENS TO THAT MAWKISH-NESS? *(Pause)*

KRAK. Children? Dead or alive?

Scene Four

Sound of whispered incantations and responses. Sections of building are lowered. NAILER *is seen kneeling on the ground.* STUCLEY *enters, holding a bible.* NAILER *stops his devotions.*

STUCLEY. Christ's cock.

NAILER. Yes . . . ?

STUCLEY. IS NOWHERE MENTIONED! *(He flings the bible at him* NAILER *ducks)*

NAILER. No . . .

STUCLEY. Nor the cocks of his disciples.

NAILER. No . . .

STUCLEY. Peculiar.

NAILER. The gospels are scrupulous in their avoidance of anatomical and physiological description. We have, for example, no image of Christ's face, let alone his—

STUCLEY. He was a man, though, wasn't he? A man, or why else did he descend to move among us?

NAILER. He was a man, yes—

STUCLEY. He was a man and I have lost five years trying to recover his dominions, five years for someone with no cock!

NAILER. He had one—
STUCLEY. He did have—
NAILER. For he was circumcised—
STUCLEY. He was circumcised, I read that, the circumcision, yes—
NAILER. Thereafter little reference, I admit—
STUCLEY. None whatsoever—
NAILER. Quite—
NAILER. What happened to it, then? *(Pause. NAILER shrugs)*
NAILER. Chastity?
STUCLEY. There is one chastity and only one. The exclusiveness of desire, not willed, but forced by passion, that's chastity. *(He walks a little)* No, this is a problem for the church, you know it is. The deity made manifest knows neither pain nor ecstasy, what use is He?
NAILER. Be careful, please . . .
STUCLEY. Careful, why?
NAILER. You may be overheard.
STUCLEY. By whom?
NAILER. You may be overheard, that's all—
STUCLEY. BY WHOM!
NAILER. By Him Who Hears All, obviously—
STUCLEY. Fuck the lunatic! (NAILER *winces. Pause)* I lay in a tent outside Edessa, while you frolicked in the English damp, while you licked the dew off widows' arses, tossed on my cot bleeding from the gums, roaring at the bowel and throat, the flux of Asia shagging me both ends, and longing to know Him, to have some sense of Him, to put my finger into Christ and feel His heat, and what pained me, what agonized me I assure you, was not the absence of a face but His castration, this Christ who never suffered for the woman, who never felt the feeling which MAKES NO SENSE. *(Pause)* He can lend no comfort who has not been all the places that we have. *(Pause)* And then of course, I knew He had, and we'd been tricked. *(Pause)*
NAILER. Tricked . . .?
STUCLEY. I am of the opinion Christ slagged Magdalene. *(Pause)*
NAILER. There is no reference—
STUCLEY. No reference, no—
NAILER. Or any indication in the gospels that I—
STUCLEY. There wouldn't be, would there?
NAILER. But all the—
STUCLEY. NEUTERED—BISHOPS—RIPPED—IT—OUT. (NAILER *stares at him)* You restore it.
NAILER. Me?
STUCLEY. Yes. Fetch a book.
NAILER. Now?
STUCLEY. Why not now? *(He shouts off)* BOOK!
NAILER. It is not in character, as I understand Him, He should have exploited his position with the woman to—
STUCLEY. Exploited? Why exploited? The thing's called love.
NAILER. She had known sex, had traded flesh, but through Christ's pity, came to the spiritual—

STUCLEY. Yes! And by His cock communicated that! (HUSH *enters with a volume and ink*) Down there, kneel, quick! (NAILER *takes the pen, kneels*) Christ finds the Magdalene—you write—He sees and pities her—and pitying her, finds her beautiful—get this down quick—put the illuminations on it afterwards or we'll be all night—

NAILER. I wasn't doing the—

STUCLEY. The mob's dispersed—He raises her—He holds her hands, her hands which have fondled knobs and money, these hands all fresh from fornication He takes in His . . . *(Pause)*

NAILER. Yes?

STUCLEY. Where were we?

NAILER. Mani habitat—

STUCLEY. Mani habitat?

NAILER. Her hands in His—

STUCLEY. No, put this in English!

NAILER. English?

STUCLEY. Yes, this is the Gospel of the Christ Erect! (*He is inspired again*) And by His gentleness, touches her heart, like any maiden rescued from the dragon gratitude stirs in her womb, she becomes to Him the possibility of shared oblivion, she sheds all sin, and He experiences the—IRRATIONAL MANIFESTATIONS OF PITY WHICH IS—*(Pause. He looks at* NAILER, scrawling) Tumescence . . . *(Pause)* Got that?

NAILER. Yes . . .

STUCLEY. Now, we are closer to a man we understand, for at this moment of desire, Christ knows the common lot. *(Pause)* And she is sterile.

NAILER. Sterile?

STUCLEY. Diseased beyond conception, yes. So that they find, in passion, also tragedy . . . (NAILER *catches up, looks at* STUCLEY) What use is a Christ who has not suffered everything? *(He wanders a little)* They say the Jews killed Christ, but that's nonsense, the Almighty did. Why, did you say?

NAILER. Yes . . .

STUCLEY. Because His son discovered comfort. 'Oh, Father, why hast thou forsaken me?' Because in the body of the Magdalene He found the single place in which the madness of his father's world might be subdued. Unforgivable transgression the Lunatic could not forgive . . . *(Pause. STUCLEY is moved by his own perceptions. He dries his eyes)* You see, how once Christ is restored to cock, all contradictions are resolved . . .

NAILER. The Church of Christ the Lover . . .

STUCLEY. Yes, why not? *(Pause. NAILER is inspired)*

NAILER. Therefore—therefore—the missing symbol of communion is—is—

STUCLEY. What?

NAILER. Milk! Body, blood and semen!

STUCLEY. Oh, luscious bishop of the new born church! *(He shouts)* Bring him his hat! *(He turns to* NAILER) Put this out, then, from your box, up the little stairs and leaning over them, put out the agonized virility of Christ! Fetch him his hat!

HUSH. What hat?

STUCLEY. I don't care what hat, bring a hat! (*To* NAILER) Begin, today I bring you hope, all you who have no hope—that's everybody—today I bring you satisfaction, all you who have no satisfaction—that's everybody again—Christ is rescued from his enemies! Make out there's been a thousand year conspiracy—what's that?

HUSH (*carrying a tool bag*). Couldn't find a hat, but this—*(He holds it upside down, shrugs)*

STUCLEY. Yes—Yes! Place it on him, crown him! (NAILER *looks uncomfortable.* HUSH *puts the bag on* NAILER'*s head)* Oh, yes, oh, look at that! The dignity, the patter, and the aged mush! All creases, not of wisdom, but repented filth, but who knows that? I'd think to look at him, oh, terrible hours in the celibate cell! DON'T TELL ME I CAN'T ORDAIN YOU, that is taking your new enthusiasm to excess, I ordain you, I ordain you, first among episcopates of Christ the Lover, I ordain you, I ordain you, etcetera, look—*(He dismisses* HUSH *with a gesture)* I must pay the builder and you have to help. (*Pause*)

NAILER. Help? I've no—

STUCLEY. He thinks I'm asking him to turn his pockets out! No, I mean invoke Christ the Lover round the estate. I mean increase the yield of the demesne and plant more acres. Plough the woods. I want a further hour off them, with Christ's encouragement, say Friday nights—

NAILER. They have already given up a day to the estate—

STUCLEY. You cannot have a castle and a forty hour week! (*Pause*) Now I'm shouting. I'm shouting at God's rep! Genuflections, genuflections, I mean we cannot be defended without sacrifice. Don't they want to be safe?

NAILER. They gather on Fridays, it is the night the women talk—

STUCLEY. There has to be a stop to that. The excessive talking. Talking here is a disease. Say it offends the scriptures and will blight their wombs—

NAILER. They know full well it doesn't—

STUCLEY. LOOK, ARE YOU RECANTED OR NOT? (*Pause*)

NAILER. I only—beg to remind you—children they have had in bumper harvests here. (*Pause*)

STUCLEY. Yes. I am forever tripping over them.

NAILER. They also are a wealth.

STUCLEY. More's the pity I've no tin mine to stuff them in, but they can clear the heath—(ANN *enters. He turns on her)* We have the keep up to your horror! For some reason I can't guess the mortar is not perished by your chanting, nor do the slates fall when you wave the sapling sticks. *(He goes towards her)* As for windows, none, or fingernails in width. Stuff light. Stuff furnishings!

ANN. The cattle have been driven off the common.

STUCLEY. Yes. the common is too big.

ANN. Too big?

STUCLEY. To be misused like this. The common will be smaller and the rest given for sheep.

ANN. Sheep.

STUCLEY. You know, wool grows on them! *(He laughs, then turns)* YOU

DISCUSS THINGS LIKE A PROPER WIFE! *(Pause)* Terrible impertinence. (HOLIDAY *enters.* STUCLEY *swings on him)* Am I imagining, or is the rate of building falling off? I look out of my window and the same low, ragged outline—

HOLIDAY. Ragged?

STUCLEY. Outline in the sky, which does not double as I wish it would—

HOLIDAY. Double?

STUCLEY. Are you short-staffed or something? Of course not double but it's static—

HOLIDAY. It's not a marrow, it's a castle—

STUCLEY. It's static, I swear it is—

HOLIDAY. I have one hundred labourers and they are shifting four courses every fortnight—

STUCLEY. Yes, you have all the answers, doesn't he, all the answers, and I have only got my eyes, why don't you look me in the eyes?

HOLIDAY. I do, but briefly—

STUCLEY. Briefly, like a liar—

HOLIDAY. No, I have a thing about—

STUCLEY. Me, too, even now you are—

HOLIDAY. Yes, I am scanning upwards for the—

STUCLEY. WELL, LOOK. *(Pause.* HOLIDAY *stares him in the eyes)*

HOLIDAY. There are—scaffolding up—*(He points with a finger)* And someone—butter-fingers might—WHAT?

STUCLEY *(tearing off)*. Where's my genius? My engineer!

ANN *(to* HOLIDAY). Give up . . .

HOLIDAY. Wha'?

ANN. Give up.

HOLIDAY. She is most persuasive, I must say, with 'er monosyllables. If you must know, I would rather be erecting hospitals myself.

ANN. Do, then.

HOLIDAY *(to* BATTER, *shuffling off)*. Monosyllabic wisdom.

ANN. Do!

HOLIDAY *(turning)*. For what? Gratitude? Mix with straw and eat it? Lovely gratitude, yum, yum!

ANN. First you do it, then you see. But first, you do it.

HOLIDAY *(shaking his head)*. See first.

ANN. You can't see first. Everyone wants to see first. See afterwards. (HOLIDAY *goes out)*

BATTER *(following)*. How the drowned man crossed the swamp . . . *(Pause. She looks at* NAILER, *who is kneeling in prayer)*

ANN. What are you doing? (NAILER *mumbles)* Have you seen yourself? *(Mumbles)* Find you a mirror . . . *(She delves in her pockets)*

NAILER. All symbols can be ridiculed. On the one hand, authority is costume, but on the other—

ANN. Never mind the words, Reg, look at the—

NAILER. I don't need to—

ANN. Look—*(She holds up a small mirror)*

NAILER. Thank you, I am perfectly aware what—

ANN. LOOK! *(He looks)* What's that? *(Pause)*

NAILER. A mitre. *(Pause)*

ANN. A mitre? Reg, you have got a bag on your—

NAILER. I am sick of your wisdom! Women's wisdom! Sick of it!

ANN. Now, don't be—

NAILER. Argument, opinion, and debate! The whispering until the candle toppled in the wax—

ANN. Reg—

NAILER. Long nights of dialogue—

ANN. Reg, there is a tool bag on your head. *(Pause. He regards her with contempt)*

NAILER. Oh, you literal creature . . . It was a tool bag . . . it is no longer a tool bag, it is a badge . . . IF YOU KNEW HOW I YEARNED FOR GOD!

ANN. Which god? *(Pause, then patiently)*

NAILER. The God which puts a stop to argument. The God who says, 'Thus I ordain it!' The God who puts His finger on the sin.

ANN. Sin . . . ?

NAILER. WHY NOT SIN? *(Pause. He gets up)* And no more Reg. *(He looks at her, goes out. A wind howls over the stage)*

Scene Five

STUCLEY, KRAK, *leaning on a wind.*

STUCLEY. There never was a wind like this before! You got a buffetting, but this . . .!

KRAK. It is the relationship between the air and the mass—the wind is trapped between the towers and accelerates to three times its velocity—

STUCLEY. He's changed the climate! What can't he do? *(He takes him by the shoulders)* You Turk. You Jew. You pedant. Make it snow. KRAK *looks at him)*

KRAK. You ask a great deal of a simple engineer—

STUCLEY. No, stuff your reservations, make it snow. *(Pause)* Because you can, you ice-cold shifter of old worlds, you can . . .

Pause. Flakes of snow flurry over the stage. STUCLEY *laughs, seizing the bewildered* KRAK *and lifting him bodily in the air.*

STUCLEY. I could chuck you into space and you would circle round my system like a star, twinkling at me from that secret eye! *(He drops him)* Play snowballs with me! I did love boyhood more than anything! Play snowballs!

KRAK *(looking at the few flakes).* There is scarcely—

STUCLEY. Chase me, then! *(He turns to run.* KRAK *waits)* Oh, it is beneath his dignity . . .

Suddenly he flings himself on KRAK. *They struggle.* KRAK *asserts his superior physical strength and forces* STUCLEY *to the ground. For a moment, he threatens his life. Then he releases him.* STUCLEY *gets to his feet, amazed.*

STUCLEY. What? *(Pause)* What? *(Pause)* Could have ruptured my throat! *(He rubs the place)* I do hate men of intellect. The curtain of the intellect, the mathematics, the poetics, concealing what dog itch, I wonder. *(Pause)* That hurt, that did . . . *(Pause)* Old man . . .
KRAK. More arches.
STUCLEY. Where?
KRAK. The outer work. Double the arches. Double the ditch. *(He scrambles up, hurries out)*
STUCLEY. Builder!

He follows. Pause. SKINNER *enters with* CANT, *hands reaching for the snow.*

CANT. S'not settling . . .
SKINNER. Fuck!
CANT. Stoppin' . . .
SKINNER. Fuck and fuck!
CANT. Got some bits . . .
SKINNER. LOST MY CRAFT!
CANT. Don't say that, you got some—
SKINNER. Laid a carpet three feet deep here once!
CANT. Remember it . . . (SKINNER *covers her face. Pause)* P'raps the brew was—
SKINNER. You did the brew . . .
CANT. Maybe the toads weren't fresh enough—
SKINNER. Not the toads . . .
CANT. Or spawning—that was it! A spawning toad shall not—
SKINNER. Not the toads! Shut up about the toads. The power's gone . . .
CANT. Not gone, just—
SKINNER. Gone! *(Pause)*
CANT. I don't think you should—just because of—(SKINNER *kneels, her face covered)* Skinner? *(Pause)* Because one—
SKINNER. Leave me alone, will you? I thank you for your kindness, but—

CANT *withdraws. A heavy snowfall.* SKINNER *does not move. In the silence the sound of a metallic movement. Armoured figures appear from different directions. They congregate, are motionless.*

BALDWIN *(at last)*. The oath!
ROLAND. The oath!
REGINALD. The oath!
ALL. We do vowe no peace shall be on earth, no ear of wheat standen, no sheep with bowel in, no hutte unburn, no chylde with blood in, until such tyme we have our aims all maken wholehearte and compleate!
REGINALD. Baldwin!
BALDWIN. Here!
REGINALD. Reginald here!

BALDWIN. I see your armour, Reginald!

THEOBALD. Theobald here!

ROLAND. I see your badge! *(Pause)* The flaming cow ran with its entrails hanging out—

BALDWIN. I cut the dog in half—

THEOBALD. One blow—

BALDWIN. The dog in two halves went—

THEOBALD. The head this way—

ROLAND. Its entrails caught around a post—

REGINALD. Double-headed axe went—

ROLAND. Its entrails caught around a post—

BALDWIN. Two-handed sword went—

ROLAND. Pulled out the seven stomachs of the flaming cow—

THEOBALD. Village bell went—

BALDWIN. Cut the dog in half—

REGINALD. The head this way—

THEOBALD. Ding—

BALDWIN. Cut the boy in half—

REGINALD. Or girl was it—

THEOBALD. Ding—

BALDWIN. Eighty millimetre gun went—

THEOBALD. Ding—

ROLAND. The seven stomachs of the bowelless cow—

REGINALD. Tracer from the half-track went—

ROLAND. The cow now with no entrails went—

BALDWIN. The mounting of the Bofors went—

REGINALD. Into the rick, into the thatch— .

BALDWIN. Spent cases rattled on the deck—

THEOBALD. Or girl was it—

ROLAND. The cow now with no entrails went—

THEOBALD. Bereft of entrails—

ROLAND. Stomachless—

BALDWIN. The boy in two halves through the village went—

THEOBALD. Ding—

REGINALD. Or girl was it—

BALDWIN. The flaming messenger of our approach—

ROLAND. Barked its—

THEOBALD. Bellowed its—

REGINALD. Screamed its—

THEOBALD. Crack division—

BALDWIN. Crack division—

REGINALD. Spent cases rattled on the deck—

THEOBALD. I fear naught, Baldwin!

BALDWIN. Fear naught!

ROLAND. Encrimsoned and imbrued!

REGINALD. Down came the thatch and in the pig squeal and the woman squeal and the man squeal and the—

THEOBALD. Fear naught, Reginald!

ROLAND. Defend the right!

REGINALD. Down came the thatch!

THEOBALD. Baldwin!

BALDWIN. I see your armour! *(Silence. HOLIDAY enters)*

HOLIDAY. Yep? *(He looks around)* Somebody ask for me? *(Pause)*

SKINNER. The bricklayers are guilty, too.

HOLIDAY. Come again?

SKINNER. The bricklayers are guilty, too.

HOLIDAY *(turning away)*. No, someone asked for me . . .

SKINNER *(as he goes)*. You mustn't look up all the time.

HOLIDAY. 'ullo, advice from every quarter—

SKINNER. Because it will not come from there. *(He stops)*

HOLIDAY. What won't? *(She does not reply. He is about to go, then, looking around him)* I saw your arse . . . *(Pause)* Excuse me, but I saw your arse—you showed your arse and I—they say you don't like men—which is to do surely, with—who you 'ad to do with, surely . . . *(Pause)* Anyway, I saw your arse . . . *(He turns, despairingly, to go)*

SKINNER. All right.

HOLIDAY *(stops)*. What—you—

SKINNER. All right . . .

The walls rise to reveal the interior of a keep. Black out.

ACT TWO

Scene One

The hall, unfinished. KRAK, *in a shaft of light.*

KRAK. He wants another wall, in case the first three walls are breached. The unknown enemy, the enemy who does not exist yet but who cannot fail to materialize, will batter down the first wall and leaving a carpet of twitching dead advance on the second wall, and scaling it, will see in front of them the third wall, buttressed, ditched and palisaded, this wall I have told him will break their spirit but he aches for a fourth wall, a fourth wall against which the enemy who does not exist yet but who cannot fail to materialize will be crucified. As for the towers, despite their inordinate height he orders me increase them by another fifteen feet. A fifth wall I predict will be necessary, and a sixth essential, to protect the fifth, necessitating the erection of twelve flanking towers. The castle is by definition, not definitive . . .

BRIAN *(rushing).* RON'S 'EAD! RON'S 'EAD!

STUCLEY *(flying in).* THE BUILD—A! THE BUILD—A!

BRIAN. Took yer eyes off, Ron!

STUCLEY. His eggshell! Someone tapped it with a spoon!

BRIAN. Took 'is eyes off and down comes a brick!

BATTER *(smartly).* Was not, idiot. Found him lying in the ditch, haunches naked and dew drops on his hairy arse.

STUCLEY. What!

BATTER. Trousers down and head bashed.

STUCLEY. What!

BATTER. Woman murder.

BRIAN. Trousers down and—

BATTER. Woman murder! *(They look at him)* Well, what else, he was not pissing under scaffolding.

BRIAN. Ron would never—

BATTER. Ron would never, 'e knows. To piss would be to take your eyes off what's above, or soak your legs. No, this was woman murder, most undignified he looked—

STUCLEY. WHO WILL TRANSLATE MY BLUEPRINTS NOW!

(ANN *enters.* STUCLEY *turns on her)* Who did this, you! Oh, her mask of kindness goes all scornful at the thought—what, me? *(He swings on* BRIAN) YOU DO THE JOB! *(And to* ANN) And such a crease of womanly dismay spreads down her jaw, and dignified long nose tips

29

slightly with her arrogance—what, me? IT STOPS NOTHING, THIS. (*To* BATTER) Find the killer who tried to hinder the inevitable! *(As* BATTER *leaves, with* BRIAN) Listen, I think morality is also bricks, the fifth wall is the wall of morals, did you think I could leave that untouched? *(He turns to go, stops)* Gang meets at sunset by the camp! The password is—*(He whispers in* KRAK's *ear)* DON'T TELL! *(He goes to leave)* Gang meets at sunset and no girls! *(He hurries out. Pause)* Gravity. Parabolas.

ANN. Gravity. Parabolas. Equations. The first man's dead. Gravity. Parabolas. Equations. Are you glad? (KRAK *does not move*) Say yes. Because you are. That's why you're here. Grey head. Badger gnawed about the ears and eyes down, bitten old survivor of the slaughter, loosing off your wisdom when you think yourself alone, I know, I do know, grandfather of slain children, aping the adviser, aping the confidant, but actually, but actually, I do know badger-head, you want us dead. And not dead simply, but torn, parted, spiked on the oaks, limbs between the acorns, a real rucking of the favoured landscape, the peace when you came here made your heart knot with anger, I know, the castle is the magnet of extermination, it is not a house, is it, the castle is not a house . . . *(Pause)* I am so drawn to you I feel sick. *(Pause)* The man who suffers. The man who's lost. Success appalls me but pain I love. Your grey misery excites me. Can you stand a woman who talks of her cunt? I am all enlarged for you . . . *(He stares at her)* Now you humiliate me. By silence. I am not humiliated. *(Pause)*

KRAK. They cut off my mother's head. She was senile and complaining. They dismembered my wife, whom I saw little of. And my daughter, with a glancing blow, spilled all her brains, as a clumsy man sends the drink flying off the table. And her I did not give all the attention that I might. I try to be truthful. I hate exaggeration. I hate the cultivated emotion. *(Pause)* And you say, come under my skirt. Under my skirt, oblivion and compensation, shoot your anger in my bowel, CUNT ALSO IS A DUNGEON! *(Pause)*

ANN. Enthralling shout . . . *(Pause, then he suddenly laughs)* And laugh, for that matter . . . *(Pause, then he turns to leave)* I mean, don't tell me it is virgins that you want, the unmarked flesh, untrodden map of girlhood, the look of fear and unhinged legs of—*(He returns, slaps her face into silence. Pause)*. You have made my nose bleed . . .

Scene Two

The PROSECUTORS *descending. A court assembling.*

NAILER. Thank you for coming.
POOL. Thank you for asking me.
NAILER. The rigours of travel.
POOL. Not to be undertaken lightly.
NAILER. No, indeed. Indeed, no. His trousers were down.
POOL. So I gather.
NAILER. I do think—

POOL. The absolute limit.

NAILER. And misuse of love.

POOL. Make that your angle.

NAILER. I will do.

POOL. The trust which resides in the moment of—

NAILER. Etcetera—

POOL. Most cruelly abused. Make that your angle.

NAILER. Thank you, I will.

POOL. Fucking bitches when your goolies are out . . .

NAILER *(to the court)*. A man proffers union—albeit outside the contract of marriage—a man proffers union—albeit without the blessing of Almighty God—he offers it by tacit understanding, by signs, by words negotiates this most delicate and sacred of all—

SKINNER. *(From the dock).* ANN!

NAILER. Lays down, abandons, puts aside all those defences which the male by nature transports in his demeanour, and in the pity of his nakedness—

SKINNER. ANN!

NAILER. Anticipating the exchange of tenderness, arms outstretched for the generosity of the feminine embrace—

SKINNER. WHERE ARE YOU, YOU BITCH—no, mustn't swear—

NAILER. A crime therefore, not against an individual—not against a single man most cruelly deceived—

SKINNER. Descend to swearing—better not—

NAILER. But against that universal trust, that universally upheld convention lying at the heart of all sexual relations marital and illicit—

SKINNER. Temper and so on, no, no, no, Skinner, stop it, it's the daylight got me going—beg pardon—

NAILER. And thereby threatening not only the security of that most intimate love which God endowed man with—

SKINNER. Daylight—got me going—sorry—

NAILER. For peace and for relief but—

SKINNER. I am not ill-tempered as a matter of fact, I don't know where that idea's come from that I—and anyway I know you hate it, loudness and shouting, you do, such delicate emotions and I—THEY HAVE DONE AWFUL THINGS TO ME DOWN THERE—do my best to be—to be contained—that way you have, you—THERE IS A ROOM DOWN THERE AND THEY DID TERRIBLE THINGS TO ME—I mean my cunt which had been so—which we had made so—THANKS TO YOU WAS DEAD—so it wasn't the abuse it might have been, the abuse they would have liked it to be had it been a living thing, were it the sacred and beautiful thing we had found it out to be and—am I going on, I do go on—are you—so thank you I hated it and the more they hurt it the better I—I was actually gratified, believe it or not, yes, gratified—

NAILER. But the very act of procreation itself, which is collaborative, which is, for its success wholly dependent on—

SKINNER. They have this way you see, of relating the torture to the offence—the things they say—you wouldn't—are you in here, I can't see—put your hand up I can't—am I being reasonable enough for you, not shouting am I, actually I'm half dead—where are you sitting, I—*(She looks around)* I call it daylight but it's relative—I WANT TO SEE YOUR HAND—Can I have a stool or not? *(A* MAN *goes to fetch it)* NOT ONE WITH A SPIKE IN THE MIDDLE! They think of everything—they do—imaginations—you should see the—INVENTION DOWN THERE —makes you gasp the length of their hatred—the uncoiled length of hatred—mustn't complain though—was I complaining—was I—beg pardon—I have this—tone which—thanks to your expertise is mollified a little—*(The* MAN *returns with a stool)* WHAT DOES THAT DO, BITE YOUR ARSE? *(She looks at it, on the ground)* Looks harmless, looks a harmless little stool, boring bit of carpentry DON'T BELIEVE IT! *(She goes towards it, extends her fingers gingerly)* Spring trap! *(She leaps back)* Spring trap! Legs fly up and grip your head, seen stools like that before, didn't think I'd fall for that, did you, not really, didn't think I'd—*(She sits on it, in utter exhaustion)* You have to kill them, don't you? Death they understand. Death is their god, not love. Because after he was dead they built nothing, for one day THEY BUILT NOTHING. And because all things decay, in actual fact for one day the castle went backwards! I mean—by virtue of erosion and the usual rot—there was less castle on Monday than on Sunday! And what did that? DEATH DID! I call it death, they call it murder, they call it battle, I call it slaughter etcetera, etcetera, the word is just a hole down which all things can drop—I mean, I put a stop to him. *(Pause)* And he was quite a nice man, as far as they—there is a limit to those even of the best intentions—he talked of mutual pleasure—really, the banality! It really hurt my ears—after what we had—to talk of—MUTUAL PLEASURE—can you believe—the very words are . . . *(She dries)*

STUCLEY.   We are up against it. We are, we really are, up against it. *(He walks about)* Having hewn away two hills to make us safe, having knifed the landscape to preserve us we find—horror of horrors—THE WORST WITHIN. *(Pause, he looks at all of them)* I find that a blow, I do, I who have reeled under so many blows find that—a blow. Who can you trust? TRUST! *(He shrieks at them, the word is a thing butted at them)* I say in friendship, I say in comradeship, I say without malice YOU ARE ALL TRAITORS! *(They deny it)* Thank you, thank you, you deny it, thank you, the vehemence I love it, thank you, lovely vehemence orchestrated and spontaneous THANK YOU BUT *(Pause)* Things being what they are I have no choice, times being what they are I feel sure you understand in everybody's interest it is crucial I regard you all as being actively engaged in the planning of my murder—no, not really, not really, silly, but as a basis for—

NAILER.   Yes.

STUCLEY.   He knows! *(Pause)* I have changed my view of God. I no longer regard Him as an evil deity, that was excessive, evil, no. He's mad. It is only by recognizing God is mad that we can satisfactorily explain the random nature of—you say, you are the theologian.

NAILER.   It appears to us He was not always mad—

STUCLEY. Not always, no—

NAILER. But became so, driven to insanity by the failure and the contradiction of His works—

STUCLEY. I understand Him!

NAILER. The absurdity of attempting to reconcile the simultaneous beauty and horror of the world is abolished by the recognition of His—

STUCLEY. THEY ARE BUILDING A CASTLE OVER THE HILL AND IT'S BIGGER THAN THIS. *(Pause)* Given God is now a lunatic, I think, sadly, we are near to the Apocalypse . . . *(He turns)* Gatherings of more than three we cannot tolerate.

NAILER. The church—

STUCLEY. I exclude births, deaths and marriages! And periodical searching of all homes I know you will not wish to hinder, what have the innocent got to conceal, it stands to reason all who complain have secrets, juries are abolished they are not reliable, quaint relics of a more secure time, I sleep alone in sheets grey with tossing, I cannot keep a white sheet white, do you find this? Grey by the morning. Does anyone find this? The launderers are frantic.

BATTER. Yes.

STUCLEY. You do? What is it?

BATTER. I don't know . . . it could be . . . I don't know . . .

STUCLEY. Why grey, I wonder?

SKINNER *(stands suddenly)*. WHAT HAVE YOU DONE TO YOUR HAIR? *(Pause)* It's plaited in a funny way, what have you—IT'S VILE. *(Pause)* Well, no, it's not, it's pretty, vile and pretty at the same time, DID YOU TAKE HIM IN YOUR MOUTH, I MUST KNOW. *(Pause)* If I know all I can struggle with it, I can wrestle it to death, but not the imagined thing, don't leave anything out, OF COURSE I AM ENTITLED TO A DESCRIPTION. *(Pause)* This floor, laid over flowers we once lay on, this cruel floor will become the site of giggling picnics, clots of children wandering with music in their ears and not one will think, not one, A WOMAN WRITHED HERE ONCE. The problem is to divest yourself of temporality, is that what you do? *(She looks at NAILER)* I gave up, and longed to die, and yet I did not die. That all life should be bound up in one randomly encountered individual defies the dumb will of the flesh clamouring for continuation, life would not have it! I hate you, do you know why, because you prove to me that nothing is, nothing at all is, THE THING WITHOUT WHICH NOTHING ELSE IS POSSIBLE. *(Pause)* I am aching from my breasts to the bottom of my bowel, but that is just desire, poof! And deprivation, poof! Love and longing, poof to all of it! AM I TO BE HANGED OR DROWNED? If you haven't had love ripped out your belly, dragging half your organs with it, don't talk to me, you haven't lived! Only the suffering to pass the sentence, you, for example . . .

(She indicates STUCLEY)

STUCLEY. Tie her to the body of her victim. *(Pause)*

SKINNER. Tie her to—

STUCLEY. And turn her loose.

SKINNER *(in horror)*. Now hold on, what—

POOL. The mercy of Almighty God be—
SKINNER. What about my execution—
POOL. Be upon you now and always—
SKINNER. MY HANGING . . . !

A reverberating explosion, blackout. Running to and fro.

STUCLEY. You heard that!
BATTER. Of course I fucking heard it . . . *(Another boom)*
STUCLEY. ANOTHER ONE.
BATTER. All right, another one . . .
STUCLEY. Why?
BATTER. Can't think.
STUCLEY. What is it!
BATTER. Can't think, I said—
STUCLEY. Comes from the East, you know!
KRAK. Yes.
STUCLEY. What! *(Pause)*
KRAK. A castle.
STUCLEY. What?
KRAK. There is one. *(Pause)*
STUCLEY. There is one . . . *(A third boom)*
KRAK. You knew, and I knew, there could not be only this one, but this one would breed others. And there is one. Called The Fortress.
STUCLEY. Bigger than this . . .
KRAK. Bigger. Three times the towers and polygonal. With ravelins beyond a double ditch, which I never thought of . . . (STUCLEY *stares for a moment in disbelief)*
STUCLEY. Everything I fear, it comes to pass. Everything I imagine is vindicated. Awful talent I possess. DON'T I HAVE AN AWFUL TALENT? TALENT?
BATTER. Yes . . .
STUCLEY. What's a ravelin?
KRAK. A ravelin is a two-faced salient beyond the outerwork—
STUCLEY. I want some—
KRAK. You want—
STUCLEY. Some ravelins, yes. Say a hundred.
KRAK. A hundred—
STUCLEY. Two hundred, then! *(A fourth boom)* AND THAT NOISE, WHAT IS IT!
KRAK. The coming of the English desert . . . *(Pause)*
STUCLEY. Yes . . .
NAILER. Almighty! Almighty!
STUCLEY. Yes . . .
NAILER. Oh, Almighty, Oh, Almighty . . . !
STUCLEY. Extinction of the worthless, the obliteration of the melancholy crawl from the puddle to the puddle, from the puddle of the maternal belly to the puddle of the old man's involuntary bladder . . . Good . . . and they make such a fuss of murder . . . NOT ME, THOUGH!

He sweeps out, with the others. ANN *appears. She is pregnant. She looks at* KRAK.

KRAK. There is one. With three times the towers and polygonal. With ravelins beyond a double ditch, which I never thought of, why polygonal, to defect what, I wonder, some young expert who sits all night with his protractors, some thin German with no woman, it is the better castle—
ANN. Better—
NAILER. And the keep low, why? And banked with earth. He sleeps alone, the opposing engineer . . .
ANN. We find a rock.
KRAK. Stink of death to English woods. Hips on the fences. Flies a noisy garment on the entrail in the bracken.
ANN. I have your child in here.
KRAK. The trooper boots the bud open and sends my—*(Pause)* Said my, then . . . *(Pause. He smiles)* Error.
ANN. It is you that needs to be born. I will be your midwife. Through the darkness, down the black canal—
KRAK. WHAT ROCK?
ANN. Off the coast. A barren place with nothing to lure murder for.
KRAK. No such place.
ANN. No wealth. Nothing to draw the conqueror.
KRAK. All places will be conquered.
ANN. Useless pinnacle of gale-lashed—
KRAK. NO SUCH THING. *(Pause)* Hot pans of blazing sun, spiky rocks in frozen waters, sheep-gnawed granites in Arctic hurricanes, all pretexts for murder and screaming up the barren slopes—
ANN. ALL RIGHT, WISDOM! ALL RIGHT, LOGIC! *(Pause)* I have a child in here, stone deaf to argument, floats in water, all pessimism filtered, lucky infant spared compelling reasons why it should acquiesce in death. *(She turns to go)*
KRAK. IS THERE ANY MAN YOU HAVE NOT COPULATED WITH? *(She stops)* I wonder . . . (CANT *runs across the stage, picks up a stone, chucks it at something off)*
CANT. S'comin'! *(A second figure runs by)*
BRIAN. S - T - E - N - C - H! *(And another)*
MAN *(laughing)*. Scarper!

They turn, stare, as SKINNER *staggers in. The decayed body of* HOLIDAY *is strapped to her front. She leans backwards from her burden, a grotesque parody of pregnancy.*

SKINNER. Wind's a bastard, running ahead. And yet these walls make eddies, and running from me sometimes meet me slap! *(They stare at her)* Not dead. Been feverish, of course. And much morning sickness all times of the day . . . (ANN *turns away her head)* Lay in the bluebells, odd sight this, on my back, head turned to gasp great lungfuls of the scent and then could not get up, you'd know this, my gravity was somewhere else, legs like windmills, beetle on its back or pregnant female, you get used to it, nothing you can't get used to, FIRST HORROR. *(Pause)* Fashion of the rotted male, exclusive garment, everybody's wearing it NOT TO COPY and his organ butts against mine, would you believe, you can live without others, SECOND HORROR! Why are you pregnant all the time, other women spent their fertility decades ago, but you—been at the herbs again? (ANN *weeps with despair*) He is losing weight. If I lie still the crows take bits away, kind crows, my favourite bird they are so solitary or live in pairs not like rooks and I was fond of rooks once, no, the solitary bird is best, you have power over her, shut her up . . . (KRAK *does not move*) He hates you. You do your hair like that, and yet he hates you. Does anyone remember what this place was once? They don't, they really don't, the children say the castle has been here a thousand years.

ANN. You should go. *(Pause)*

SKINNER. Go . . .

ANN. Yes. Not hang round here.

SKINNER. Go where? I live here.

ANN. No such thing as live here any more, go where you might find peace and rub the thing off you, where you won't be stoned. *(Pause)*

SKINNER. No.

ANN. Do you like to be stoned?

SKINNER. Yes. *(Pause)* Yes to punishment. Yes to blows. *(Pause)*

ANN. What have I done to you? (SKINNER *laughs*)

SKINNER. She thinks—she has the neck—she has the gall—to think she brought me to—she has to think herself responsible! *(She looks to* KRAK) Careful! She's after your suicide! Hanging off the battlements for love! The corpse erect! Through her thin smile the knowledge even in death she got you up! *(Mimicking)* Did I do this? *(She turns to* ANN) This is my place, more stones the better and pisspans, pour on! You and your reproductive satisfactions, your breasts and your lactation, dresses forever soddened at the tit, IT DID GET ON MY WICK A BIT, envy of course, envy, envy, envy of course. I belong here. I am the castle also.

ANN. You do suck your hatreds. You do—suck—so. And he—also sucks his.

SKINNER *(as a group of hooded prisoners enters)*. That way the dungeon!

ANN. Gulls at the sewer . . .

SKINNER. Bear left and wait, the torturer's at breakfast! *(They shuffle)*

ANN. Snails on the eyes of the dead . . .

SKINNER. Tax evaders on the first rung, work-shy on the second!

ANN. Suck pessimism, suck fear . . .!

SKINNER. Don't hang about, the last lot came up again. Only some bits were missing! (ANN *hurries out. The gang shuffles further.* BATTER *appears, with a short stick*) There are eighty-seven stairs and the last two flights they throw you off!

BATTER. All right, get along . . .

SKINNER. Hullo, Bob . . .

BATTER. Wotcha, darling . . .

SKINNER. Look well . . .

BATTER. Thank you . . . *(To the gang)* 'HO SAID TO STOP?

SKINNER. Cold again . . .

BATTER. English summer . . .
SKINNER. Fuckin' 'ell . . .
BATTER *(as he passes)*. Take care . . .
SKINNER. Will do . . .

The prisoners and BATTER *depart.* SKINNER *takes an apple from her clothes and begins to eat it.* KRAK, *who has been watching in perfect stillness, suddenly kneels at her feet.* SKINNER *stops, mouth open, apple mid-air.*

SKINNER. What? *(Pause)* What? *(Pause)* What, you bugger, what?
KRAK. The Book of Cunt. *(Pause)*
SKINNER. What book is that?
KRAK. The Book of Cunt says all men can be saved. *(Pause)* Not true. *(Pause).* She pulled me down. I did not pull her. She pulled me. In the shadow of the turret, in the apex of the angle with the wall, in the slender crack of 39 degrees, she, using the ledge to fix her heels, levered her parts over me. Shoes fell, drawers fell, drowned argument in her spreading underneath . . . *(Pause)* European woman with her passion for old men, wants to drown their history in her bowel . . .! *(Pause)*
SKINNER. Scares you . . .
KRAK. My arse. My arse, she says . . . *(Pause)*
SKINNER. Yes . . .?
KRAK. Cunt you lend or rent, but arse you have to will . . . true ring of marriage . . . brown button of puckered muscularity . . . the sacramental stillness born of hanging between pain and ecstasy . . . IN SHIT I FIND PEACE IS IT! *(He scrambles to his feet)* Don't tell them I came here—
SKINNER. Tell who . . .?
KRAK. Where's cunt's geometry? The thing has got no angles! And no measure, neither width nor depth, how can you trust what has no measurements? Don't tell them I came here . . .
SKINNER. No . . .
KRAK. FIND PEACE IN SHIT, DO I? *(He looks around, goes out. HUSH enters with a dish. He places it at SKINNER's feet)*
SKINNER. Wha's that?
HUSH. Lamb.
SKINNER. What?
HUSH. Stew.
SKINNER. What? *(He starts to slip away)* It's an offence to feed me! (CANT *enters with a dish, lays it down)* What—
CANT. Baked apple—
SKINNER. You—
CANT. Can't stay! *(She withdraws, running low)*
SKINNER. Oh, God, Oh, Nature, I AM GOING TO BE WORSHIPPED.

Scene Four

KRAK *is sitting at his desk.* STUCLEY *appears.*

STUCLEY. Saw you. (KRAK *looks up*) Giving your brain away. *(Pause)* Saw you. *(Pause)* Whose brain do you think it is? (KRAK *just looks*) Well, no. Cock's free but brains are property. *(He walks a little, stops)* Deceit floats up, like fat on the tea cup. Like bones scuffed years after the murder, the knife, the stain, the knickers that refused to rot, I FOLLOWED YOU INTO THE THICKET, YES . . . ! *(Pause)* Symposium of military architects. Twigs cracked but did they look, twigs shattered but did they look? Crouching with diagrams you might have slammed the doors of Asia and they would not have budged. SUPREME CONCENTRATION OF TREASONABLE GENIUS. Are you listening or not?

KRAK. Drawn cunt. *(Pause)*

STUCLEY. What?

KRAK. In 27 versions.

STUCLEY. The diagrams you traded with the Fortress, were they approximate or comprehensive, did they include the order of defence, the sally ports, which entrances were blind and which lead to the keep, HOW SAFE ARE WE AFTER THIS? (KRAK *holds up his drawing*) The representation of that thing is not encouraged by the church. *(Pause. He is looking at it)* It's wrong, surely, that—*(Pause)* I have never looked at one, but that—

KRAK. Gave him all my drawings. And got all his. They are experimenting with a substance that can bring down walls without getting beneath them. Everything before this weapon will be obsolete. This, for example, is entirely redundant as a convincing method of defence—

STUCLEY. What—

KRAK. Its vertical profile, which I took further than any other architect, renders it utterly vulnerable . . .

STUCLEY. What—

KRAK. It goes up, instead of down. Is high, not wide. Is circular and not oblique. Is useless, in effect and an invitation to—

STUCLEY. ONLY JUST FINISHED IT. *(Pause)*

KRAK. Yes . . . *(He returns to his drawing)*

STUCLEY. DON'T DRAW CUNT. I'M TALKING! *(Pause)* This is a crisis, isn't it? Is it, or isn't it? You sit there—you have always been so—had this—manner of stillness—most becoming but also sinister—dignity but also malevolence—easy superiority of the captive intellect—IS THAT MY WIFE'S BITS—I wouldn't know them—what man would—I know, you see— I am aware—I do know everything—I do—I think you have done this all to spite me—correct me if I'm wrong—

KRAK. Spite—

STUCLEY. Spite me, yes—

KRAK. Spite? I do not think the word—unless my English fails me—is quite sufficient to contain the volume of the sentiment . . . *(Pause)*

STUCLEY. You blind draughtsman . . . all the madness in the immaculately ordered words . . . in the clean drawings . . . all the temper in the perfect curve . . . *(He pretends to flinch)* MIND YOUR FACES! DUCK HIS GUTS! INTELLECTUAL BURSTS! *(Pause)* Tumescent as the dick which splits, splashing the ceiling red with sheer barminess, NIGEL! *(Pause)* But I'm not spited. If you do not feel spited no amount of spite can hurt you, Christ was the same, NIGEL! *(Pause)* We burn people like this. Who give away our secrets. Burn them in a chair. Fry them, and the fat goes—human fat goes, spit . . .! Does—spit! (ANN *enters*) No. Nigel I want. *(She looks at them)* Violence not abundance.

ANN. The ease of making children. The facility of numerousness. Plague, yes, but after the plague, the endless copulation of the immune. All these children, children everywhere and I thought, this one matters, alone of them this one matters because it came from love. But I thought wrongly. I thought wrongly. *(Pause. She looks at KRAK)* There is nowhere except where you are. Correct. Thank you. If it happens somewhere, it will happen everywhere. There is nowhere except where you are. Thank you for truth. *(Pause. She kneels, pulls out a knife)* Bring it down. All this. *(She threatens her belly. Pause)*

STUCLEY. You won't. *(Pause)* You won't because you cannot. Your mind wants to, but you cannot, and you won't . . .

Pause. He holds out his hand for the knife. She plunges it into herself. A scream. The wall flies out. The exterior wall flies in. In a panic, SOLDIERS. Things falling.

Scene Five

A haze of light.

SOLDIER ONE. Raining women!

SOLDIER TWO. Mind yer 'eads!

SOLDIER ONE. Raining women!

NAILER. The temper of the Almighty, who gave you abundance, imagine His temper! Standing before Him how will you say I did destroy that which it was not mine to dispense with—

SOLDIER TWO. Mind yer 'eads! *(A fall)*

NAILER. The spirits of your unborn children will rise up in accusation saying—

SOLDIER TWO. AND ANOTHER!

NAILER. Oh, wickedness to so wantonly cast off the gift of life—*(A fall)*

BATTER. These bitches will put paid to the race . . .

SOLDIER ONE. TO YER RIGHT!

NAILER. I cast thee out, saith the Lord, I cast thee from my sight—

SOLDIER ONE. TO YER RIGHT!

SOLDIER TWO. ANOTHER!

NAILER. STOP IT! STOP IT OR ELSE . . .! *(A fall)* Oh, contempt, contempt of life!

BATTER *(looking up)*. That's it, that's it for today . . .

SOLDIER TWO. No more for today . . . *(The SOLDIERS wander off. CANT appears)*

BATTER *(To CANT)*. All right, get on with this . . .

NAILER *(rising to his feet).* They must be locked away. All women who are pregnant. Chained at wrist and ankle, like cows in the stall. They bear our future in their innards and they kill it. BY WHAT RIGHT! All women big about the middle, lock up! *(He hurries out. CANT straightens the limbs of the fallen)*

BATTER. Not theirs, birth. Not theirs, is it?

CANT. Dunno.

BATTER. Theirs only, I mean. What's your opinion?

CANT. No opinion.

BATTER. Go on, I won't tell.

CANT. No opinion! *(She carries on)* Death is not yours, either.

BATTER. Wha'?

CANT. Not yours only, is it? Not an opinion.

CANT. Come again . . .

CANT. We birth 'em, and you kill 'em. Can't be right we deliver for your slaughter. Cow mothers. Not an opinion. (KRAK *enters. He moves among the fallen)*

KRAK. Warm women, cooling . . . *(He stops by another)* Cooling women . . .

BATTER. Husbands want to kill 'em. Want to murder 'em, but they are murdered. Not finding anything to take revenge on, go barmy, mutilate the flesh they simpered over once . . . *(Pause)*

KRAK. She undressed me . . . *(They look at him)* I lay there thinking . . . what is she . . . what does she . . . undressed me and . . . *(Pause)* What is the word?

BATTER. Fucked?

KRAK. Fucked! *(He laughs, as never before)* Fucked! *(Pause)* Went over me . . . the flesh . . . with such . . . inch by inch with such . . . *(Pause)* What is the word?

CANT. Desire. *(He stares at her, then throwing himself at her feet, tears open his shirt, exposing his flesh to her)*

KRAK. Show me.

CANT. Wha'?

KRAK. That!

CANT. Show—

KRAK. Desire! *(She hesitates)*

BATTER. Go on . . . *(She puts her hand out, touches him unwillingly, mechanically)*

KRAK. Not it . . .

CANT. Trying but I—

KRAK. Not it!

CANT. Can't just go—

KRAK. NOT IT! NOT IT!

She runs out. KRAK shudders. STUCLEY enters, looks at him.

STUCLEY. Lost love . . .! Nothing, nothing like lost love . . . *(He rests a hand on KRAK's bent head)* And she was of such sympathy, such womanly wisdom I could not bring myself, for all the damage she had done me, bring myself to take revenge, any man would, you say, yes, any man would! Not me, though . . .! *(He draws KRAK's head to his side)* And you, dear brother in lost love, I UNDERSTAND. The very substance of the body wilts, like dummies who have lost their straw, we flop! Oh, I know, I know his filetting, I TOO WAS FILETTED. And all the valley sobs with grief, shh! *(He cups his ear)* The howl of men bereaved . . . odd sound among the trees, oh, extraordinary brotherhood! *(Pause)* The new walls will be so low they cannot jump off. Not fatally. They will roll down the slopes only and—*(He stops, looking from one to another. They stare at him)*

BATTER *(at last)*. Come for a walk . . .

STUCLEY. A walk?

BATTER. Through the meadows. Through the trees.

STUCLEY. Rather not.

BATTER. Rather not . . . *(He looks about him)* Just like Jerusalem, when we got in, the women were thick on the steps and clotting up the doors, you trod the rolling carpet of their flesh, oh, intoxication! Rather not, he says!

STUCLEY *(resisting)*. WHAT'S THIS WALK EXACTLY!

BATTER. And you were up there, first always, up the ladders—

STUCLEY. Was I? Dangerous . . .

BATTER. Dangerous, yes, England and—

STUCLEY. Saint George! YOU'RE PUSHING ME WHERE I DON'T WANT TO GO. (BATTER *sweeps him up in his arms*)

BATTER. And light! So light, do you find that? *(The* SOLDIERS *make no move)* Light as a child . . . *(He walks through them, and out.* KRAK *scrambles to his feet)*

KRAK *(to the soldiers)*. His last walk. His last walk. *(They ignore him)* Listen, his last walk . . .! *(He offers himself)* Cut the skull through, will you! The one with the axe? Slice it round the top and SSSSSSS the great stench of dead language SSSSSSS the great stench of dead elegance dead manners SSSSSSS articulation and explanation dead all dead YOU DON'T HOLD WOMEN PROPERLY IN BED.

An effect of rain and time

Scene Six

SKINNER, *festooned with the skeleton, outside the walls.* BATTER *enters, with* NAILER. *Pause.*

BATTER. The Church of Christ the Lover. Fuck it.

SKINNER. What?

BATTER. New church. Tell her.

NAILER. The Holy Congregation of the Wise Womb.

BATTER. All right? *(Pause. She looks at them)*

NAILER. Christ, abhorring the phallus, foreswore his maleness, chose womanly ways. Scripture in abundance for all this.

BATTER. All right?

SKINNER. I don't like wombs.

BATTER. You don't like—

SKINNER. Hate wombs. *(Pause.* BATTER *looks to* NAILER)

BATTER. She hates—

NAILER. I have been up sixteen hours assembling a theological foundation for all—

BATTER. All right—

NAILER. NOT ALL RIGHT. *(Pause)* We acknowledge the uniquely female relationship with the origin of life, the irrational but superior consciousness located in—

SKINNER. Sod wombs—

NAILER. Do listen, please! *(Pause. He proceeds)* The special sensitivity of woman to the heart-beat of the earth—Romans, VIII, verses 9 to—

SKINNER. He does go on—

NAILER. 17, which hitherto has held no special place in doctrine but which henceforward will be—

SKINNER. PALAVER OF DISSIMULATORS!

NAILER.   The foundation of the edict LET THERE BE WOMANLY TIMES! *(Pause)*

BATTER. Wha'd yer think? *(Pause)* Well, do you wanna church or not? *(Pause)*

SKINNER. She was all womb. Tortured me with her fecundity, her moisture, birthing, birthing, very public, down among the harvest, crouches, yells, and slings it round her neck, where did I leave my sickle, oh, blood on her knees and afterbirth for supper, and me like the arid purse of rattling coins, to her whim and feminine mood of the moon stuff danced my service, and then stabs it, STABS IT, THE VANITY OF IT! *(Pause)* No womb lover me. Witches' blight if I could manage it. I won't help you govern your state, bailiff made monarch by a stroke of the knife... *(Pause)*

BATTER. No . . . *(Pause)* You govern it instead. *(She quivers)*

SKINNER. Now wait—now wait a minute—WAIT! Are you—DON'T TEASE ME . . .!

NAILER. He is in a positive lather of good faith—

SKINNER. Some limp joke or spiteful provocation—

NAILER. None, I—

SKINNER *(grabbing* NAILER *by the collar)* WHAT...! WHAT...

NAILER.   You—are—hurting—my—throat—

SKINNER *(releasing him).* Some bastard—some twisted—scratch my brain I can't—fingers at the old seat of suspicion—what's your—YES! YES! *(Pause)* Wait a minute, wait, what's your—get me swelling, get me gloating, dangle it before her eyes—she blobs about the eyes, the eyes are vast and breath goes in and out, in-out, in-out, pant, pant, the bitch is hooked, the bitch is netted, running with the water of desire GIVE ME POWER WHAT FOR, look at me, all twitching with the appetitie for— *(Pause)* All right yes . . . *(Pause.* NAILER *tosses down the castle keys.* SKINNER *looks at them, then with a lightning movement, snatches them off the ground)* EXECUTE THE EXECUTIONERS! *(She leaps)* All my pain, all my violence, all my scars say—hear my scars, you—SUFFERING TO BE PAID OUT, DEBTS EXTRACTED, SETTLEMENT IN YELLS! Oh, she is not dignified, she is not charitable, the act of kindness from the victim to the murderer, grey eyes serene in pain absorbed, agony knitted into cloths of wisdom WHO SAYS! Reconciliation and oblivion, NO! GREAT UGLY STICK OF TEMPER, RATHER *(She turns on her heel)* Nobody say it's all because I'm barren! I have had children, I have done my labour side by side, and felt myself halved by her spasms, my floor fell out with hers and yes, I haemhorraged *(Pause. They stare at her. She goes to the wall, runs her hand over the stone)* I can't be kind. How I have wanted to be kind. But lost all feeling for it . . . Why wasn't I killed? The best thing is to perish in the struggle . . . *(She turns to* BATTER *and* NAILER) No. *(She tosses the keys down)* I shall be too cruel . . .

KRAK. Got to.

SKINNER. Who says?

KRAK. Got to! *(Pause. She looks around)*

SKINNER. Out the shadows, who thinks the only perfect circle is the cunt in birth . . . (KRAK *emerges from a cleft in the wall)*

KRAK. Demolition needs a drawing, too . . . *(Pause)*

SKINNER. Demolition? What's that? *(A roar as jets streak low. Out of the silence,* SKINNER *strains in recollection)* There was no government . . . does anyone remember . . .there was none . . . there was none . . . there was none . . .!

Scenes from An Execution

SCENES FROM AN EXECUTION was first broadcast on BBC Radio 3 on 14th October, 1984, with the following cast:

GALACTIA	Glenda Jackson
CARPETA	Clive Merrison
URGENTINO	Freddie Jones
SUFFICI	Clifford Rose
RIVERA	Darlene Johnson
OSTENSIBLE	Peter Howell
PRODO	David Sinclair
THE SKETCHBOOK	Brett Usher
SUPPORTA	Elizabeth Rider
DEMENTIA	Helena Breck
SORDO	Anthony Hall
PASTACCIO	Brett Usher
OFFICIAL	Peter Acre
MAN IN THE NEXT CELL	John Strickland
GAOLER	Peter Acre
LASAGNA	Mark Straker
FIRST SAILOR	Anthony Hall
SECOND SAILOR	Mark Straker
THIRD SAILOR	David Sinclair
WORKMAN	Anthony Hall
Directed by	Richard Wortley

Scene One

A studio in Venice.

THE SKETCHBOOK.   The sketchbook of the Venetian painter Galactia lying on her parted knees speaks of her art, speaks of her misery, between studies of sailcloth in red chalk the persistent interruption of one man's anatomy . . . On every margin where she has studied naval history his limbs or look intrude, the obsession alongside the commission . . .

GALACTIA.   Dead men float with their arses in the air. Hating the living, they turn their buttocks up. I have this on authority. Their faces meanwhile peer into the seabed where their bones will lie. After the battle the waves were clotted with men's bums, reproachful bums bobbing the breakers, shoals of matted buttocks, silent pathos in little bays at dawn. The thing we sit on has a character. Yours says to me KINDNESS WITHOUT INTEGRITY. I don't think you will ever leave your wife.

CARPETA.   I shall leave my wife, I have every intention of leaving my—

GALACTIA.   No, you never will. I believed you would until I started this drawing, and now I see, your bum is eloquent on the subject, it is a bum that does not care to move . . .

CARPETA.   I resent that, Galactia—

GALACTIA.   You resent it—

CARPETA.   I resent it and I—

GALACTIA.   Resentment is such a miserable emotion. In fact it's not an emotion at all, it's a little twitch of self-esteem. Why resent when you can hate? DON'T MOVE!

CARPETA.   You are the most unsympathetic, selfish woman I have ever had the misfortune to become entangled with. You are arrogant and vain and you are not even very good looking, in fact the contrary is the case and yet—

GALACTIA.   You are moving—

CARPETA.   I couldn't care if I am moving, I have my—

GALACTIA.   You are spoiling the drawing—

CARPETA.   I have my pride as well as you, and I will not lie here and be attacked like this, you have robbed me of all my resources, I am exhausted by you and my work is going to the—

GALACTIA.   What work?

CARPETA.   I HAVE DONE NO WORK!

GALACTIA.   Carpeta, you know perfectly well you only stand to benefit from the loss of concentration you have suffered through loving me. You have painted Christ among the flocks eight times now, you must allow the public some relief—

CARPETA. YOU DESPISE ME!

GALACTIA. Yes, I think I do. But kiss me, you have such a wonderful mouth.

CARPETA. I won't kiss you.

GALACTIA. Please, I have a passion for your lips.

CARPETA. No, I will not. How can you love someone you despise?

GALACTIA. I don't know, it's peculiar.

CARPETA. Where are my trousers?

GALACTIA. I adore you, Carpeta . . .

CARPETA. I AM A BETTER PAINTER THAN YOU.

GALACTIA. Yes—

CARPETA. FACT.

GALACTIA. I said yes, didn't I?

CARPETA. And I have painted Christ among the flocks eight times not because I cannot think of anything else to paint but because I have a passion for perfection, I long to be the finest Christ painter in Italy, I have a longing for it, and that is something an opportunist like you could never understand—

GALACTIA. No—

CARPETA. You are ambitious and ruthless—

GALACTIA. Yes—

CARPETA. And you will never make a decent job of anything because you are a sensualist, you are a woman and a sensualist and you only get these staggering commissions from the state because you—

GALACTIA. What?

CARPETA. You—

GALACTIA. What?

CARPETA. Thrust yourself!

GALACTIA. I what?

CARPETA. Oh, let's not insult each other.

GALACTIA. Thrust myself?

CARPETA. Descend to low abuse—

GALACTIA. IT'S YOU WHO—

CARPETA. I am tired and I refuse to argue with you—

GALACTIA. Get out of my studio, then, go on, get out—

CARPETA. Here we go, the old Galactia—

GALACTIA. You are such a hypocrite, such an exhausting, dispiriting hypocrite, just get out—

CARPETA. As soon as I've got my trousers—

GALACTIA. NO, JUST GET OUT.

PRODO *(entering)*. Signora Galactia?

CARPETA. I want my—

GALACTIA. No! Ask your wife for some trousers, she'll make you some trousers, down on her knees, eye to the crutch, sew, sew, sew, little white teeth nipping the thread—

CARPETA. We can't go on like this, can we? We can't go on like this—

GALACTIA. Snip, snip, snip, lick, lick, lick—

PRODO. Signora Galactia?

GALACTIA. I HATE YOU, YOU ARE RUINING MY LIFE. *(Pause, then the door slams)* I am losing my mind. My mind is breaking up and drifting in all directions, like an ice field in some warm current, hear the crack, drifting blocks of consciousness that took me forty years to put together, I look ten years older and I already looked old for my age, I cannot let myself be splintered like this, can I? I cannot! Who are you? What do you want?

PRODO. I'm Prodo, the Man with the Crossbow Bolt In His Head.

GALACTIA. Oh, yes.

PRODO. Come at two o'clock, you said.

GALACTIA. Yes . . .

PRODO. It is two o'clock.

GALACTIA. Yes . . .

PRODO. I am prompt because I am in demand. Where there is no demand, there is no haste. I would appreciate it if we got on, I am required by a Scotch anatomist at half past three.

GALACTIA. Yes.

PRODO. The fee is seven dollars but no touching. I also have an open wound through which the movement of the bowels may be observed, and my hand is cleft to the wrist, if you're interested. I suggest two dollars for the bowel, and the hand you can look at with my compliments. It is a miracle I am alive, I am a walking manifestation of organic solidarity and the resilience of the Christian state. Shall I proceed?

GALACTIA. Please.

PRODO. I will take my hat off. Are you ready?

GALACTIA. Ready. *(Pause)*

PRODO. Voila. The tip is buried in the centre of my brain and yet I suffer no loss of faculties. Pain, yes, and alcohol may occasion blackouts. The shaft may be observed, to twitch perceptibly at times of mental exertion. If you would care to set me a simple arithmetical sum I may be able to exhibit this phenomenon.

GALACTIA. Incredible . . .

PRODO. Go on, ask me.

GALACTIA. Seven times eleven.

PRODO. No, simple, simple.

GALACTIA. Twelve plus five.

PRODO. Twelve plus five is . . . is . . .

GALACTIA. It's moving . . .!

PRODO. Is seventeen! There is no other recorded evidence of a man sustaining traumatic damage to the brain of this order and retaining consciousness. Would you care to examine the bowel?

GALACTIA. Why not, while we're at it?

PRODO. I do not normally reveal this to a woman.

GALACTIA. Try not to think of me as a woman. Think of me as a painter.

PRODO. I will think of you as a painter. Are you braced for the exposure? I will lower my belt.

GALACTIA. Good God . . .

PRODO. Please do not faint.

GALACTIA. I am not going to faint . . .

PRODO. The passage of undigested material along the alimentary canal by the process known as peristalsis can be clearly observed. The retention of the bowel within the pelvic cavity is sometimes problematic given the absence of a significant area of muscularity.

GALACTIA. Spilling your guts . . .

PRODO. As you wish. That is nine dollars, please.

GALACTIA. Are you bitter, Prodo?

PRODO. Bitter?

GALACTIA. For being left a specimen?

PRODO. God gave me life. God led me to the battle. God steered the bolt, and in his mercy turned my maiming to my benefit. That is nine dollars, please.

GALACTIA. Unbuttoning yourself in rich men's rooms . . .

PRODO. Thank you.

GALACTIA. Grotesque celebrity. Shudder maker. Clinging like a louse to dirty curiosity . . .

PRODO. Do you require a receipt?

GALACTIA. What about the battle, Prodo?

PRODO. I do not talk about the battle. Thank you. One dollar change.

GALACTIA. Oh, come on, I love your wounds, but tell me how you got them.

PRODO. A treatise on my condition is to be published in the Surgical Gazette. I am also featured on a box of matches, one of which I leave you as a souvenir. I hope you have enjoyed the trivial interest of my misfortune—

GALACTIA. Paint your pain for you.

PRODO. Oh, bloody hell, it's raining—

GALACTIA. Your butchery.

PRODO. Is there a short cut to the Rialto?

GALACTIA. Paint your anger. Paint your grief.

PRODO. I'll see myself out, thank you—

GALACTIA. IDIOT. *(Pause)*

PRODO. What?

GALACTIA. Holding your bowel in. With an arrow sticking out the middle of your head. IDIOT. *(Pause)*

PRODO. If you'll excuse me, I—

GALACTIA. I am painting the battle, Prodo. Me. The battle which changed you from a man into a monkey. One thousand square feet of canvas. Great empty ground to fill. With noise. Your noise. The noise of men minced. Got to find a new red for all that blood. A red that smells. Don't go, Prodo, holding your bowel in—

PRODO. WHAT SORT OF WOMAN ARE YOU?

GALACTIA. A midwife for your labour. Help you bring the truth to birth. Up there, twice life-size, your half-murder, your half-death. Come on, don't be manly, there's no truth where men are being manly—

PRODO. Don't trust you, got a mad eye—

GALACTIA. Shuffling away there, stop, will you?

PRODO. Afraid of you.

GALACTIA. Afraid of me? Me? Why?

PRODO. Hurt me—

GALACTIA. Never—

PRODO. Ruin it—

GALACTIA. What? *(Pause)* What!

PRODO. MY PEACE WITH LIFE.

GALACTIA. Listen. Listen, look at me, look at me, what sort of a face do I have? Look at it, is it a good face? Is it generous?

PRODO. It's all right—

GALACTIA. No, it's more than all right, it's a good face, it's an honest face, broad and generous—

PRODO. Yes—

GALACTIA. Of course it is, I know it is and so do you, I know my face, I paint it, over and over again, I am not beautiful and I wouldn't be beautiful if I could be—

PRODO *(sarcastically)*. No, you wouldn't be—

GALACTIA. I tell you I would not, I do not trust beauty, it is an invention and a lie, trust my face, I am a woman who has lived a little, nothing much, I have not been split up the middle like you have, but I have picked up a thing or two and I tell you I have never been at peace with life, I would not be at peace with life, there is no such thing and those who claim they have it have drugged their consciences or numbed their pain with futile repetitions of old catechisms, catechisms like your patter, oh, look at you. WHO DID IT TO YOU, PRODO, AND WHAT FOR? I will paint your violence for all the passing crowds who mock your daft appearance... (PRODO *sobs*) There, there . . . we must be brave . . .

PRODO. Nightmares . . .

GALACTIA. Yes . . . yes . . .

PRODO. Down the bottom of the sheets all arms and legs . . .

GALACTIA. Go on . . .

PRODO. Bones going . . . air full of cracking bones . . . oars going . . . bones going . . .

GALACTIA. Yes . . .

PRODO. Flesh falling down . . . flesh raining down . . . bits going . . . everywhere bits going . . . rain of bits and THIS TUMULT IN MY BED . . .!

GALACTIA. Oh, my poor ridiculous man, I shall paint the why of all your terrors, shall I?

PRODO. Give me back my little peace . . .

GALACTIA. Why was the battle fought, Prodo?

PRODO. My little ease, you—

GALACTIA. Why? *(Pause)*

PRODO. Freedom, of course.

GALACTIA. Freedom . . .

PRODO. Glory, of course.

GALACTIA. Glory . . .

PRODO. The Honour of the Great Republic and the Humiliation of the

Pagan Turk!

GALACTIA.   Oh, look, the arrow's twitching! Round and round it goes . . .

PRODO.   DOESN'T!

GALACTIA.   Twirling, feathered thing, oh, look!

PRODO.   DOESN'T!

GALACTIA.   Wonderful man, grappling with dim truths!

PRODO.   What are you trying to do to me, Signora! *(Pause)*

GALACTIA.   Truth, that's all, just truth. See yourself out, will you?

PRODO.   You are an unkind woman, you . . .

GALACTIA.   Thank you for coming.

PRODO.   Digging out my—

GALACTIA.   Sketchbook! Sketchbook! Where have I—

PRODO.   Horror of my—

GALACTIA.   Laid it down and—

PRODO.   STUPID LIFE.

GALACTIA.   Good bye.

SKETCHBOOK.   The upper left hand corner shows a parting in the angry sky; the clouds have opened and sun bursts through the aperture, flooding the canvas and highlighting all the subjects that lie under the slanting beams, a dramatic diagonal that draws the eye, pulls the eye down jerky surfaces of battle and through passing horizontals to—

Scene Two

A palace in Venice.

URGENTINO.   I can't see my brother. *(Pause)*

GALACTIA.   You can't see your—

URGENTINO.   Well, of course I can see him, don't be obtuse. Obviously I can see him, I mean I cannot see *enough* of my brother. I like my brother and I want to see more of him. He is the Admiral and he is not big enough.

GALACTIA.   He is—fourteen feet high. *(Pause)*

URGENTINO.   Listen, I do hope we are going to become friends.

GALACTIA.   Me too.

URGENTINO.   I like to be friends with everybody. It is a weakness of mine. But if we are to be friends I think we have to understand one another. I know you are an artist and I am a politician, and we both have all sorts of little mannerisms, turns of speech, beliefs and so on, which neither of us will be happy to renounce, but for the sake of easy communication may I suggest we stop the little dance of personal regard and concentrate on facts? Simple, incontrovertible facts? My brother is Admiral of the Fleet and he does not occupy a prominent enough position in this drawing. There! Do you like my jacket? It's damascene.

GALACTIA.   It's very fine.

URGENTINO.   It is fine. I take clothes very seriously.

GALACTIA.   I admire that in a man.

URGENTINO.   Do you! We are going to get on! I pride myself on my good taste, and my good taste extends to artists too. You know Carpeta almost got this job? The cardinals on the fine art committee were hot for him.

GALACTIA.   Is that so?

URGENTINO.   I fought them bitterly. I said he is spent. He is spent, isn't he? Utterly.

GALACTIA.   He is only thirty-five.

URGENTINO.   What does it matter if he's seventeen? He's spent. Listen, I know artists pretend to be kind to one another, but be honest, you all hate one another's—

GALACTIA.   That isn't actually the case—

URGENTINO.   No, no, of course not, but when it comes down to it you—

GALACTIA.   No. Actually. No.

URGENTINO.   You won't admit it. I like that. All right, you won't admit it! Signora, I have taken a chance with you, do you know why? Because you sweat. Your paintings sweat. Muscle. Knuckle. Shin. No drapes in your pictures. They clash. Kissing even, is muscular. You see, I have eyes, I look, but also I smell, I smell your canvas and the smell is sweat. Do you find me offensive? I am a devotee.

GALACTIA.   I rejoice in your appreciation.

URGENTINO.   Good! But listen, this is a state commission, an investment, an investment by us, the Republic of Venice, in you, Galactia. Empire and artist. Greatness beckons, and greatness imposes disciplines. Do you like these grapes? They come from Crete. We left two thousand soldiers dead there, but we have the grapes. Little bit of sand. Little bit of history.

GALACTIA.   What are you trying to say to me?

URGENTINO.   I am saying you have not been asked to paint the back wall of the vicarage. I am saying that a canvas which is one hundred feet long is not a painting, it is a public event.

GALACTIA.   I know that. It's why I'm here.

URGENTINO.   Good! You are ambitious, and ambition is a fine thing, but it involves changes of perspective. My brother is quite big enough, but is he in the right place? That is what I meant when I said I could not see my brother. I have a sense of humour, you see!

GALACTIA.   Yes, yes—

URGENTINO.   You see!

GALACTIA.   I also have a sense of humour—

URGENTINO.   Signora, obviously you have a sense of humour, only an artist with a sense of humour would place the Admiral of the Fleet in such an obscure position! For all his size, he does not dominate the drawing. Now, that is very witty of you, but you see, I am witty, too, so let's be serious, shall we?

GALACTIA.   Are you faulting me for composition?

URGENTINO.   Signora Galactia! Would I do such a thing? You are the artist! I only remind you of certain priorities. A great artist must first of all be responsible, or all his brush strokes, and all his colouring, however brilliant, will not lift him out of the second rank.

GALACTIA.   I am painting the Battle of Lepanto. I am painting it in such a

way that anyone who looks at it will feel he is there, and wince in case an
arrow should fly out of the canvas and catch him in the eye—

URGENTINO. Excellent!

GALACTIA. So that children will tremble at the noise and cling to their
parents as the ships collide—

URGENTINO. Excellent!

GALACTIA. Such a noisy painting that people will stare at it holding their
ears, and when they have dragged themselves away, look at their clothes to
see if they have been spattered with blood or brain—

URGENTINO. Marvellous! You see, you are passionate, you are magnifi-
cent!

GALACTIA. Make them breathless, make them pale!

URGENTINO. Yes! Yes! But also make them PROUD.

GALACTIA. Proud?

URGENTINO. Great art will always celebrate! Celebrate, Celebrate! Do
you love Venice, Signora Galactia?

GALACTIA. I am a Venetian.

URGENTINO. So you are, but—

GALACTIA. I have said, I am a Venetian.

URGENTINO. Then praise Venice. I think I need say no more than that.
Bring me another drawing soon.

Scene Three

A disused barrack in the Arsenal.

SUPPORTA. It's cold in here!

GALACTIA. Paint in gloves.

SUPPORTA. Paint in gloves?

GALACTIA. If you concentrate hard enough you'll forget the tempera-
ture. Anyway, it won't always be winter.

DEMENTIA. It stinks.

GALACTIA. Of what?

DEMENTIA. Men. There is a proper male stink in here.

GALACTIA. Of course. It used to be a barracks.

DEMENTIA. Vile.

GALACTIA. It is absolutely the right smell for the subject. If you are
painting soldiers, you should live among soldiers.

DEMENTIA. It is disgusting coming here. If you wear a coloured scarf
they take you for a prostitute.

GALACTIA. Wear black.

DEMENTIA. Why should I wear black? I'm not a widow.

GALACTIA. Listen, I asked to come here. When I asked for a place big
enough to paint in I was offered all sorts of things, even a museum. But
who wants to paint in a museum? Live among what you are painting,
among who you are painting. Look at their faces, the way they move. You

will never be anything but drapery painters if you do not want to look. I have tried to make you look since you were children. The habit of looking. Come here, look through the window.

SUPPORTA.   I don't want to climb up on—

GALACTIA.   No, look! The way they walk, the soldiers. It is not a walk, is it? It is a hip thrust, a pelvic deformation. Hip and thigh, the stiff buttock and the contorted face. The soldier when he is not dying . . . *(Pause)* Enjoy looking and stop thinking everyone wants to fuck you.

DEMENTIA.   They do not pester you, you are an old woman!

GALACTIA.   All right, nothing's proper, nothing's right! But it's a free room and you can get a hundred feet of canvas in it!

DEMENTIA.   Male groin. Male swagger.

GALACTIA.   I don't know why it frightens you. I never brought you up like it.

DEMENTIA.   Doesn't *frighten* me.

GALACTIA.   I was kissing at seven and gave birth at twelve.

SUPPORTA.   Here we go—

GALACTIA.   I had twelve lovers by my fifteenth birthday—

DEMENTIA.   Oh, God, mother—

GALACTIA.   For all that I knew nothing until I met Carpeta, nothing! At forty-six I find—I knew nothing. And Carpeta is spineless. Pity.

WORKMAN *(calling off)*. Signora!

SUPPORTA.   The scaffolders have finished.

DEMENTIA.   There really isn't enough light in here.

GALACTIA.   It's the afternoon.

DEMENTIA.   There's still not enough light—

GALACTIA.   Painters make too much of light. I can work by a candle.

DEMENTIA.   There's no light, it stinks and I—

GALACTIA.   Dementia, if you do not wish to be involved in this run away and look after your children—

DEMENTIA.   Now, don't be silly, I am only saying—

GALACTIA.   Go on, run away and—

DEMENTIA.   Why do you have to be so—

WORKMAN *(approaching)*.   Finished it, Signora—

GALACTIA.   Children's piss and husband's dinner, clean underwear and dinner party stuff, go on!

DEMENTIA.   Why is she—

GALACTIA.   So many people wanting—what—what is it?

WORKMAN.   Finished the scaffolding. *(Pause)*

GALACTIA.   Let me see. *(Pause)* No, you didn't listen to me.

WORKMAN.   Three tiers, you said—

GALACTIA.   I said three tiers—

WORKMAN.   An' that's what you—

GALACTIA.   What do you think I am? Do you think I am a monkey? How am I supposed to crawl along—

WORKMAN.   'ho said you were a monkey? I never said you were a—

GALACTIA.   Got to stand up there for six or seven hours, do you—

WORKMAN.   Remind you what you said, you—

SKETCHBOOK.   The sketchbook of the fifth daughter of the painter Galactia, known as Supporta, also an artist and scenery painter, in red chalk, shows her mother sitting with her legs apart, mouth hanging open like a rag, remonstrating with workmen in a vast room empty but for stools and scaffolding . . .

Scene Four

GALACTIA's *studio.*

GALACTIA.   Do you like my flesh, Carpeta? Tell me you do, although it's coarse and the pores are dark as pepper. Aren't I all colours? White eyelids, mottled on my shoulders, blue veined in my thigh and red veined on my cheeks? Are you fascinated by me? I have a sort of sagging basket of flesh where my children have swung, and my navel protrudes like a rude tongue. But my tongue! You love that, don't you, restless tongue! Do I exhaust you? Oh, God, I exhaust him, he has a weary look . . . *(Pause)* I want to show the effect of cutlasses on flesh, the way they slice out pieces, like a melon, flinging the scrap into the air. It is not something I shall ever see, but I imagine it. It is not important to witness things. I believe in observation, but to observation you must lend imagination. The Doge says I am to submit to him another drawing in which the Admiral is given greater prominence. Well, I shall do. I shall show him not only prominent but RESPONSIBLE. And a face which is not exulting but INDIFFERENT. No, let go of me, you always start to touch me when I think, what are you afraid of, don't you like me to think? You see, you feel my breasts as if—I INSIST ON THINKING even though you have your finger—WHAT IS IT YOU OBJECT TO? *(Pause)* What? *(Pause)* Oh, come on, you—
CARPETA.   I have been displaced.
GALACTIA.   By what?
CARPETA.   The battle.
GALACTIA.   Rubbish.
CARPETA.   I have been. I am not on your mind.
GALACTIA.   Of course you are on my mind—
CARPETA.   Not all the time!
GALACTIA.   No, not all the time, how can I—
CARPETA.   You see! Not all the time!
GALACTIA.   Oh, God . . Oh, God, Carpeta . . . *(He sobs)*
CARPETA   You make me—utterly childish . . .
GALACTIA.   Yes . . .
CARPETA.   Clinging . . . rag . . .
GALACTIA.   I wish I were not sensual. I wish I had not got from my mother, or my father was it, this need to grasp and be grasped, because it drives me into the arms of idiots who want to crush me. Wonderful, idiotic crushing in the night. Can't you just crush me in the night? I am very happy to be crushed

in bed but I am a painter and you can't have that off me. Oh, don't sulk, please don't sulk, there really isn't time for all this mending and accommodating to your sensitivity, which in any case isn't really sensitivity, it's brutality, but never mind that—

CARPETA.   It is not brutality, it is possession—

GALACTIA.   All right, you say it's—

CARPETA.   IT IS NOT BRUTALITY.

GALACTIA.   No . . . all right . . .

CARPETA.   I am humiliated by my feelings for you. Humiliated. *(Pause)*

GALACTIA.   Carpeta, how do you paint pity? You've always painted pity, and I never have. Tell me how to do it.

CARPETA.   I don't think you could paint pity, Galactia.

GALACTIA.   Why?

CARPETA.   I don't think you have pity, so you can't paint it.

GALACTIA.   Ah. Now you're being spiteful.

CARPETA.   No. You are violent, so you can paint violence. You are furious, so you can paint fury. And contempt, you can paint that. Oh, yes, you can paint contempt. But you aren't great enough for pity.

GALACTIA.   Great enough?

CARPETA.   It's hard luck on you, because if you could paint pity, the Church would stand up for you, and if you could paint glory, you would have the State. But you will please nobody.

GALACTIA.   You know what I think? I think you are marvellous at honouring yourself. Marvellous. But pity's got nothing to do with greatness. It's surrender, the surrender of passion, or the passion of surrender. It is capitulating to what is. Rather than pity the dead man I would say—there—there is the man who did it, blame him, identify. Locate responsibility. Or else the world is just a pool, a great pool of dirty tears through which vile men in boots run splashing. You paint pity very well, but you endure everything, and in the end you find Christ's wounds—enticing. You find suffering—erotic. Your crucifixions—there is something wrong with them. They love them in the Church, the bishops wet themselves with appreciation, but really they are rather dirty pictures, Carpeta. And if you were normal, you would love a younger woman.

Scene Five

The barracks.

SKETCHBOOK.   Painting the Turk.

GALACTIA.   I scoured Venice for a Turk. I could not find a Turk, but I discovered an Albanian.

DEMENTIA.   The Albanian is staring at me. Will you ask him not to stare at me.

GALACTIA.   He sells pineapples on San Marco. Look at his eyes!

DEMENTIA.   I do not wish to see his eyes.

GALACTIA.   Perfect head. Rotund, male head . . .

DEMENTIA.   He is rubbing himself and staring at me. DO KEEP STILL!
GALACTIA.   At first I thought, paint him dead. With arms flung out and
backwards, falling headlong from the Muslim deck, and then I thought,
what a waste of a head, because who will look at a head which is upside
down? DO STOP WHATEVER IT IS YOU ARE DOING, YOU WILL
MAKE MY DAUGHTER ANGRY. So instead I did a suppliance. I did a
figure begging for his life, and I put him at the feet of the great Admiral,
with his palms extended, and I thought I would put into his expression the
certain knowledge he would be murdered on the deck. So with one figure I
transformed the enemy from beast to victim, and made victory unclean.
And I suspect, even as I draw it, they will hate this . . .!
SUPPORTA.   Can I say something?
GALACTIA.   Mmm . . .
SUPPORTA.   I am your daughter and I love you.
GALACTIA.   Yes . . .
SUPPORTA.   But I am also a painter, and old enough not to flatter you.
GALACTIA.   Yes . . .
SUPPORTA.   And I know, as you do, that you are the best painter in
Venice.
GALACTIA *(stops sketching).*   Have you noticed this, I wonder, that when
someone is about to pay you a crippling and devastating compliment, they
always preface it by saying they are not going to flatter you. What do you
want?
SUPPORTA.   You always spoil things.
GALACTIA.   Do I?
SUPPORTA.   Have to prove something. Superior insight, incisive wit.
Whatever. I want to talk to you.
GALACTIA.   I'm sorry. Yes.
SUPPORTA.   It doesn't matter how they patronize you, or attack you for
your promiscuity, you are still the best painter in Vencie, and if you were
not promiscuous, but severe, prudish and had no appetites at all, they
would use that against you, they will always have to find something be-
cause you are brilliant and a woman.
GALACTIA.   What are you trying to say, Supporta? The preamble is very
comforting but what exactly—
SUPPORTA.   You have this vast commission in front of you, which will
prove beyond all argument what you are, and I am frightened you will
waste it. *(Pause)*
GALACTIA.   Waste it.
SUPPORTA.   Yes. You will offend, and when people are offended, they
cannot see the brilliance, only the offence.
DEMENTIA.   I feel I am being burned here. Burned by eyes. I am going out
to mix some paint. Look at it, sticks to you, sticky little Albanian thing!
(She goes out)
GALACTIA.   Go on.
SUPPORTA.   Give the people what they want, and they will love you. They
will exclaim over you. And after that, no woman painter here will have to
struggle against prejudice, because you will have proved us. You see, I

think you have a responsibility—not to the State, but to Venetian women. Paint your feelings, by all means, that is your power, but let the public in, share with them. The drawing of the Turk insults them.

GALACTIA.   You want me to paint like a man.

SUPPORTA.   No—

GALACTIA.   Yes, you want me to paint a man's painting.

SUPPORTA.   I do not. What man can paint like you in any case? The vigour, the effort, the agony? No man.

GALACTIA.   And no man honestly hates murder, either. You ask me to be responsible, when what you really mean is, 'celebrate the battle!'

SUPPORTA.   I am thinking of you.

GALACTIA.   Oh?

SUPPORTA.   I am thinking how mean life is, how it gives you one bite only. Think how they'll attack you, they'll say this woman scorns us, mocks our sacrifice. You scour your own mind, you hunt down your own truth, but perhaps you're vain, too, not to compromise. Maybe you're arrogant, have you thought of that?

GALACTIA.   Arrogant, me?

SUPPORTA.   You joke, but—

GALACTIA.   Supporta, listen to me. The act of painting is an act of arrogance. It is arrogant to describe the world and then to shove the thing into the world's face. It is arrogant to compete with nature in painting a flower, or to challenge God by improving views. To paint is to boast, and if you don't like boasting you ought not to paint. Now, let me concentrate. I will negotiate with power because I have to. I will lick the Doge's crevices if need be, because he has power. I am not wholly an idiot and I like to eat and drink as well as you. MUSTAFA I MAY BE TALKING BUT I AM WATCHING YOU. Look at him, he can't sit still if Dementia is out of the room, fidgets like a ferret in the trousers—

SUPPORTA.   You will not listen to advice, will you?

GALACTIA *(to the Albanian).*   It's all right, she's coming back! Do look at him!

SUPPORTA.   You are adamantly self-opinioned and—

GALACTIA.   Here she comes, look at her waist, her lovely waist—

DEMENTIA.   Will you not encourage him!

GALACTIA.   His eyes, look! Look at his eyes, isn't he amazing?

SUPPORTA.   INTOLERABLE. *(Pause)*

GALACTIA.   The Turk thinks he will die. How does he know he will die? Because the Admiral's expression is bereft of mercy, is a mask of—

Scene Six

The Admiralty.

SKETCHBOOK.   Painting the Admiral. *(A clock ticks in the room)* The preliminary sketch. *(Pause)*

SUFFICI. Do you like my face?

GALACTIA. Well, that's a bold question.

SUFFICI. I like bold questions.

GALACTIA. Normally they ask it in a different way. They say 'Is my face difficult to draw?' *(Pause)* It is difficult to draw.

SUFFICI. I have always been painted—cravenly.

GALACTIA. How do you mean, cravenly?

SUFFICI. The real me not attempted.

GALACTIA. What is the Real You? *(Pause)* Come on, what's the Real You?

SKETCHBOOK. The Admiral of the Atlantic, the Admiral of the Two Seas, the General of the Home and Distant Waters, is shown leaning on a desk with one fist underneath the chin, staring with a melancholy gaze into the middle distance, in red ink, the victor of Lepanto in civilian dress, patrician forehead weary from high office, he is—

SUFFICI. A homosexual gardener.

GALACTIA. You're teasing me.

SUFFICI. Garacci guessed it, and painted my fingers on the nuzzles of my dogs in such a way that all the armour in the world could not conceal my nature . . .

GALACTIA. Garacci is superficial.

SUFFICI. I felt, for all the steel in which I was encased, naked. He is wonderful with hands, don't you think?

GALACTIA. I cannot stomach Garacci.

SUFFICI. My hands said The Warrior Prefers the Living Flesh. In no uncertain manner. But who looks at hands?

GALACTIA. They will look where they are told to look, where the composition compels their attention. I do hands better than Garacci, you'll see. Everyone will see the hands, it will be a hand painting, the hands of the killed, the hands of the killers hands red to the wrists, hands without owners. Can you think of anything more pitiful than a severed hand? Or eloquent? I think it is the ultimate in pity. My lover says I have no pity, but you don't have to have Christ hanging off a tree trunk to show pity, do you? Hands are the points of contact between man and man, man and woman, the instruments of friendship, symbols of love and trust. And in battles they drop from the sky, and men shake stumps in anger, don't they? Raw things prodding. I must say I am furious to find you like this, so gentle and so subtle, I am drawing badly. I am drawing rubbish—

SUFFICI. Don't I keep still enough?

GALACTIA. Yes, terribly still, terribly dignified. I did not see you in the victory parade, I do not go to victory parades, I have only seen Garacci's portrait, and I thought it slavish and flattering, but I come here with my book and pencils, and blow me down, you have to hand it to him, he's done you right, you have the most compassionate face I've ever seen. Silly me, I should know the world is full of contradiction, but it's thrown me. See first, and look after. I saw you, and then I looked, and the two don't tally. Never mind, it must be that I'm not looking deep enough. *(A page is ripped from the sketchbook)* Start again.

SUFFICI.   From this window you can see the Fleet.

GALACTIA.   Yes.

SUFFICI.   Riding at anchor. Do you care for ships?

GALACTIA.   I have spent a fortnight drawing them.

SUFFICI.   Do you like them?

GALACTIA.   The trader, in a good wind, bringing things, yes.

SUFFICI.   And the warships?

GALACTIA.   No.

SUFFICI.   Why did the committee choose you, Signora, to paint the Battle of Lepanto?

GALACTIA.   Because I do what no one else can. I paint realistically. Either that or the papers got mixed up.

SUFFICI.   I feel sure they made the wise choice.

GALACTIA.   Oh, now, don't be generous, sitting so still there with your grey eyes resting on your empire . . . *(Pause)*

SUFFICI.   I think you are rather angry with me . . .

GALACTIA.   Grey eyes with no chink for doubt to enter, only the little veiling of the lazy lid, the droop of bedroom miseries . . . *(Pause)*

SUFFICI.   Go on . . . *(Pause)* My drooping eyelid? *(Pause)* Go on, I am not offended . . .

GALACTIA *(refusing)*.   Sometimes you have to admit they get things right, the bureaucrats; for all their corrupt deliberations, they pick an artist who might just TELL THE TRUTH. And then God help us, it's blood and mayhem down the cold museums.

SUFFICI.   My eyelid.

GALACTIA.   I don't know whether Venice is a good republic or a bad one, I am not political—

SUFFICI.   Me neither, what about my—

GALACTIA.   The moment you go in for politics, you cavil, you split up the truth—

SUFFICI.   Please—*(Pause)*

GALACTIA.   I go from my belly. Yes or no. And when I show meat sliced, it is meat sliced, it is not a pretext for elegance. Meat sliced. How do you slice meat? *(Pause)*

SUFFICI.   I think you are, for an artist, rather coarse.

GALACTIA.   Coarse for an artist? It's an artist's job to be coarse. Preserving coarseness, that's the problem.

SUFFICI.   And simple. By which I do not mean unintelligent. I mean there are things you choose not to know.

GALACTIA.   Such as that Admirals like to run naked among flowers? I do know that.

SUFFICI.   I mean, the Necessary War, and the Unnecessary war.

GALACTIA *(sarcastic)*.   Ah, now you are stretching me . . .

SUFFICI.   You see, you mock so! So replete with your own belief, you bustle and assail me, you lend no space to opposition, or risk yielding me some credibility. You see the eyelid droops, but you are afraid of it, afraid to be sucked down into the well of a different truth. You have seen me, but you are not looking. They told me you were a better painter.

GALACTIA. Your sensitivity. Your great, swaggering sensitivity. Do not look at the armour, look at the fingers. Do not look at the sword, look at the eyelids. Ignore the blood, think of the buttocks in the garden. *(Pause)* Sorry, no.

URGENTINO *(entering).* I interrupt! Philistine bore invades the sitting!

SUFFICI. We were not progressing . . .

URGENTINO. I was passing Ponte Dore on my way to the Treasury and who do I meet, I meet Gina Rivera, distinguished critic, poet and sensualist, and I say at once, damn economics, didn't I, damn economics, let us creep into the admiralty and see how artists work!

RIVERA. Yes.

URGENTINO. Look, her sketchbook on the floor, all hot with smudges and corrections, Gina, look! Touch it! Can she touch it?

GALACTIA. Why not?

URGENTINO. A critic should watch a painter. How many critics witness the moment of production? None! They let fly at the finished canvas and know nothing of its history! By the way, Signora, the latest sketches are superb, they are perfect, I wish you to proceed at once to the painting. My brother is big enough.

GALACTIA. Good.

URGENTINO. Gina, finger the book, finger it, the smell of it! I am a fetishist for art, forgive my infantile enthusiasm!

RIVERA. The composition for the battle is most original, Signora.

GALACTIA. Yes, I try to be original.

RIVERA. You cannot try to be original. Either you are or you are not, surely?

GALACTIA. No, originality is as much an effort as anything else. It is sweated for, unfortunately.

RIVERA. It's inspiration, surely? You cannot labour for brilliance—

URGENTINO. Suffici, listen! Two of the most remarkable women in Venice, divorced, promiscuous and combative!

RIVERA. I am not divorced. It's you that is divorced.

URGENTINO. It is absurd that the critic and the artist are not better related, absurd! You are utterly dependent on one another and yet you squirm with mutual suspicion!

RIVERA. The critic is afraid of the artist and envies her power. She is ashamed of what she secretly believes to be an inferior gift, that of exposition. So instead of serving the artist, she humiliates her.

URGENTINO. There, that is a bad critic. There are good ones, too.

RIVERA. Of course.

SUFFICI. Signora Galactia has had a trying morning, coping with my face.

URGENTINO. What is wrong with his face? He has a lovely face!

GALACTIA. Yes.

URGENTINO. What I should like for my brother is this—clemency in victory, modesty in triumph, virtue in—

SUFFICI. Do shut up.

URGENTINO. All right, I leave him to your imagination! But show him for what he is—a tactical genius.

RIVERA. How does she do that? Show him holding a compass?

URGENTINO. Yes.

RIVERA. In the middle of a battle?

URGENTINO. Why not?

RIVERA. Because she is a realist.

URGENTINO. All right, she is a realist! I don't understand these terms.

RIVERA. It means she paints what happened.

SUFFICI. There is no such thing as what happened, surely? Only views of what happened. Just as there is no such thing as a man. Only images of him. *(Pause)*

URGENTINO. Excellent! Signora, I shall forever be dropping in your studio. It is the nature of a good patron that he shows his curiosity.

GALACTIA. I do not welcome visitors as a rule.

URGENTINO. I am not a visitor, as a rule. But this is not a private commission. It is the gold and silver of the Venetian people on your paintbrush, is it not? We must be off, we have had our treat. *(Pause)*. Listen, listen! The murmur of the fleet, the whack of the wind in the canvas, that is a beautiful sound, the sound Odysseus heard as he kipped on his deck with dirty sailors . . . I spent three years in the Navy, didn't I? Didn't I? Cesare?

SUFFICI. Yes . . .

URGENTINO. Yes, he says. Eloquent yes. I was the Great Naval Disaster. But Cesare is a Great Man, a great, Great Man. We had different mothers, unfortunately. Come on, Gina, let's get out from under the genius's feet.

RIVERA. How do you paint a Great Man, Signora?

GALACTIA. I'm not sure, Signora. I know the conventions, of course.

RIVERA. The conventions, yes, of course . . . *(They depart. Pause)*

GALACTIA. Carry on, shall I? *(Pause)* No? *(Pause)* Oh, now don't say you're not going to speak . . .! *(Pause)* All right, don't speak . . .

Scene Seven

Inside a church. A priest intones a funeral oration.

CARPETA. I don't think you should stand next to me.

GALACTIA. Not stand next to you?

CARPETA. In public.

GALACTIA. What?

CARPETA. Shh.

GALACTIA. I don't understand. If I sleep with you I don't see—

CARPETA. Shh.

GALACTIA. EVERYBODY KNOWS WE—

CARPETA. Please, this is a colleague's funeral! *(Pause)*

GALACTIA. He wouldn't have objected. He was never in his wife's bed, either.

CARPETA. I should be very grateful if you'd—

GALACTIA. It's funny but a funeral is calculated to make me want to fuck—

CARPETA. Please—

GALACTIA. Not fuck, exactly—mate.

CARPETA. I shall move away from you.

GALACTIA. You know, heat to heat, the procreative, mindless dog and bitch thing down the—

CARPETA. I am standing over there—

GALACTIA. DON'T DARE MOVE.

CARPETA. You are hurting my—

GALACTIA. I haven't finished yet—

CARPETA. My wrist, you—

GALACTIA. All right, go! *(Congregational responses)*

CARPETA. Please, why are you following me?

GALACTIA. Do you know what I hate?

CARPETA. No, and I don't—

GALACTIA. I hate the way you act in public. It disgusts me. Is it because you are a religious painter?

CARPETA *(to a bystander).* Excuse me—

GALACTIA. Who do you think you are fooling? The way you stick your nose up in the air, and your eyes go all—

CARPETA. Excuse me, excuse me—

GALACTIA. I know you have to please your patrons, but really! Farini hated all this, and so do I.

CARPETA. His wife wanted it. She wanted a proper funeral.

GALACTIA. She would have done. She hated him.

CARPETA. Nonsense.

GALACTIA. She could not dispose of him in life so she—

CARPETA. Shh!

GALACTIA. Catch Farini with a crucifix—hey, Sordo—

MOURNER. Shh!

GALACTIA. Sordo, imagine the old man watching this! We do terrible dishonour to dead men. And he was an atheist!

MOURNER. Be quiet!

GALACTIA. Fact! He was investigated by the Inquisition—

MOURNER. Rubbish.

GALACTIA. In 15—

MOURNER. Rubbish.

GALACTIA. Oh, do stop saying rubbish, he was a great painter and he couldn't stick God, I should know, he taught me.

SORDO. That isn't true.

GALACTIA. No?

SORDO. It isn't true, Galactia, that he—

GALACTIA. All right, correction, he wasn't a great painter, he was a moderate painter and he hated God. Is that better? I was being generous because he's dead.

SORDO. Galactia, you are drunk.

GALACTIA. Oh, God . . . !

SORDO. You are drunk and everyone—

GALACTIA. Why is it you cannot speak the truth without someone saying you must be drunk? That or barmy? They put Farini in the madhouse for saying the Pope could not tie his own shoelaces—*(Protests)* They did— FACT! He recanted. *(More groans and complaints)* I must get some fresh air. All this death worship is getting up my nostrils, where's my lover? Oh, look at him, he has the face of—now I see it, Carpeta's Christ paintings are self-portraits! And half an hour ago he had his mouth—*(Shouts of protest)* All right, I'm going! *(The door closes. Sounds of the street)* A dead painter, claimed. The dissenting voice, drowned in compliments. Never happier than when lying in the gutter with a bricklayer, drunk out of mind. Human, warm, and round. And yet a frightful liar. Couldn't put a brush to paper without lying—the happy poor, the laughing rags of tramps and scabby dogs pawing the dirt. Guilty old fornicator . . .

CARPETA. I wish you wouldn't do that.

GALACTIA. What?

CARPETA. Exhibit yourself.

GALACTIA. Is that what I do?

CARPETA. Yes.

GALACTIA. I thought I was keeping death at bay.

CARPETA. No, why do you—

GALACTIA. They worship death because, listen—

CARPETA. WHY DO YOU? WHY? *(Pause)*

GALACTIA. I don't know . . . I don't know . . . I am not happy, Carpeta, which is why I laugh so much. *(Pause)* I must work now.

CARPETA. Come home with me, my wife—

GALACTIA. I left Dementia finishing the oarsman's cuff, I want to see she—

CARPETA. My wife's at the—

GALACTIA. Your wife . . . *(She laughs a little)*

CARPETA. Come home with me—

GALACTIA. GET OFF. *(Pause)*

CARPETA. It is all right for you to finger me in public, murmuring things in churches, naughtiness and descration, but when I—

GALACTIA. Yes—

CARPETA. When I ask for what I—

GALACTIA. Absolutely—

CARPETA. What I—

GALACTIA. EGOTISTICAL AND MONSTROUS WOMAN. *(Pause)* Yes.

Scene Eight

The barracks. A door slams.

SKETCHBOOK. Painting the Dying. The dead and dying occupy one third of the entire canvas, which is no less than six hundred and sixty six square feet, an area not strictly in accordance with the sketch submitted to the authorities. They lie sprawled, heaped and doubled against gunwales and draped over oars, with expressions of intolerable pain, and by a method of foreshortening, their limbs, attached and unattached, project uncomfortably towards the viewer . . .

GALACTIA. Who's there? Oh, come on, who's—Look, I only have to call and—

RIVERA. Working late, Signora?

GALACTIA. People choose the most extraordinary times to visit you.

RIVERA. Candles . . . the incense of the pigment . . . rather a religious atmosphere . . .

GALACTIA. Is it.

RIVERA. A woman alone in a barracks.

GALACTIA. Not really alone. There are several hundred marines within shouting distance.

RIVERA. You squat up there like—skirts pulled up like—perched on your scaffolding—a full and undone breast—these nights are hot, I couldn't hold a brush for sweating, do you sweat, Signora? And the oil which trickles down. You have got smudges of burnt umber on your cheek.

GALACTIA. It's not umber, it's sienna.

RIVERA. I have just come from church. Do you like churches? The whispering of women! 'Lord, make me pregnant!' 'Lord, stop me being pregnant!" Women pleading, women dragging their pain up to the altar, and I thought, I must see Galactia, and there you are, sleeves rolled up like a plasterer . . . superb. The Doge is terribly unhappy. I thought I'd tell you.

GALACTIA. Yes.

RIVERA. You know.

GALACTIA. Yes. He visits me, and he feels sick. He is frightened I will paint some awful truth. So he walks up and down, and looks. And feels sick. *(Pause)* No fun being a doge.

RIVERA. Are you interested in politics?

GALACTIA. No.

RIVERA. May I tell you a little about politics, or would it spoil your concentration?

GALACTIA. Yes.

RIVERA. I'd like to anyway. *(Pause)* The Doge is actually a highly responsible patron of the arts. Dilettante, of course, and slightly vulgar. But then, to someone of your sensibilities, all patrons are vulgar, I expect. He loves artists, and the harder he loves them, the more vulgar he becomes, it's all rather pitiful, really, but—

GALACTIA. Bang goes the concentration. *(Pause)*

RIVERA. Sorry. The point is this. The Doge is insecure. It would not take a great deal to have him removed from office.

GALACTIA. Doges come, and doges go . . .

RIVERA. It isn't as simple as that, unfortunately.

GALACTIA. Isn't it?

RIVERA. There is a climate very favourable to painting here. To poetry, to sculpture. It is a climate that permitted the appointment of a controversial painter like yourself to represent the greatest triumph of Venetian history—

GALACTIA.   Represent what?

RIVERA.   The greatest triumph of Venetian—

GALACTIA.   I think you've come to the wrong studio. On my contract it says—I can't find the contract at the moment but it says—I'm sure it says—'The Battle of Lepanto.' Nothing about triumphs of—triumphs of what?

RIVERA.   The doge has taken an extraordinary risk in commissioning you. If you humiliate him, you aid his enemies and invite his fall. And if he falls, there will be a new incumbent, and I assure you, as someone who is interested in politics, none of the other candidates cares one iota for—

GALACTIA.   You're a critic, aren't you?

RIVERA.   Yes, but I must have something to criticize. *(Pause)*

GALACTIA.   Excuse me, this figure of a man dying of wounds sustained during the greatest triumph of Venetian—

RIVERA.   IT ISN'T THAT SIMPLE. *(Pause)* I make no attempt to influence you on points of style, I only—

GALACTIA.   The muscle hanging off the bone is rather difficult to do with you—

RIVERA.   DIRTY MESS OF TRUTHS, SIGNORA, CLINGING TO THE MOUTH. *(Pause)* It is really beautiful in here, and the candles catch your eyes. I am not ashamed of what I tell you, bringing world of muck against your doors. Absolutely not ashamed. How beautiful my clothes are, and my whiteness, most impeccable woman, drifting through galleries. But it is very violent, criticism. A very bloody, knocking eyeballs thing. Knives out for slashing reputations, grasping the windpipe of expression. I try to look nice, though it's murder I do for my cause. Good night. *(She withdraws)*

GALACTIA.   Sitting through the dark, thirty feet aloft on creaking boards, with moths gone barmy round the candles, someone's got to speak for dead men, not pain and pity, but abhorrence, fundamental and unqualified, blood down the paintbrush, madness in the gums—

VOICES OF THE CANVAS.   The Dying—The Dying—

GALACTIA.   The Admiral is a hypocrite. Humility my arse.

VOICES OF THE CANVAS.   The Dying—The Dying—

GALACTIA.   Algebraic. Clinical. Shrivelled testes and a sour groin.

VOICES OF THE CANVAS.   The Dying—The Dying—

GALACTIA.   The soldier does not smell his own lie but repeats the catechism of the state, bawling pack of squaddies yelling male love— .

VOICES OF THE CANVAS.   THE DYING! THE DYING!

GALACTIA.   The painter who paints for the government recruits the half-wit and stabs the baby in its mess—

THE VOICES OF THE CANVAS.   THE DYING! THE DYING!

FIRST SAILOR.   OI! *(Silence. Three drunk sailors have come in)* Woman up a ladder . . .

SECOND SAILOR.   Anybody seen my bed?

GALACTIA.   This is out of bounds to naval personnel, will you—

FIRST SAILOR.   Oi! *(Pause)* Woman up a ladder . . .
GALACTIA.   You will kick the paint jars over—
SECOND SAILOR.   Seen my bed!
GALACTIA.   You have kicked them over, stupid!
SECOND SAILOR.   Beg pardon, looking for my—
THIRD SAILOR.   'ho are you callin' stupid?
SECOND SAILOR.   Not a bed . . .
GALACTIA.   Who is your commanding officer?
SECOND SAILOR.   Table, not a bed . . .
THIRD SAILOR.   'ho is she callin' stupid?
GALACTIA.   You have come to the wrong door, this is not a barracks, it's
   a—
FIRST SAILOR.   Oi!
GALACTIA.   studio and I—
FIRST SAILOR.   Oi! *(Pause)*
SECOND SAILOR.   Wha'? *(Pause)* Christ . . .!
SKETCHBOOK.   The sketchbook shows three seamen variously disposed
   about a massive canvas, mouths open, hands hanging at their sides. One of
   them holds a bottle loosely in his hand, as if, out of sheer amazement, he
   has forgotten to be drunk . . . *(The bottle splinters)*
THIRD SAILOR.   MUR-DER!
FIRST SAILOR.   Daggers! Rifles! Arms!
SECOND SAILOR.   ATT-ACK! ATT-ACK!
FIRST SAILOR.   Christ and the Republic, Ho!
GALACTIA.   DO NOT STAB THE CANVAS!
SECOND SAILOR.   Fire! Fire!
FIRST SAILOR.   Look out, be'ind yer!
THIRD SAILOR.   HELP! HELP!
FIRST SAILOR.   Guard yer backs! *(The sailors rampage)*
SECOND SAILOR.   Cut-lass!
GALACTIA.   Mind that tray of—*(A pile of bottles is scattered)*
FIRST SAILOR.   Slash the bugger!
THIRD SAILOR.   MUR-DER! MUR-DER!
GALACTIA.   MIND MY PALETTES, YOU—*(A collapsing table and
   items)*
SECOND SAILOR.   Blood!
FIRST SAILOR.   GOT-CHA!
THIRD SAILOR.   AAAGGHHH!
GALACTIA.   GET OUT! GET OUT OF HERE, YOU—
FIRST SAILOR.   Ow! She 'it me!
GALACTIA.   OUT! OUT! *(With whoops, two of the sailors run out.
   Pause)* And you.
SECOND SAILOR.   I think—I think—
GALACTIA.   Look at this mess . . .! How am I to work when you—when
   people like you—look at it!
SECOND SAILOR.   I think I—

GALACTIA. Do you have any idea of the cost of these things? Have you?
SECOND SAILOR. Think I—
GALACTIA. Twenty dollars for an ounce of that, you—
SECOND SAILOR. Go and—
GALACTIA. Lunatics, I'll—
SECOND SAILOR. Be sick . . . *(Pause)*
GALACTIA. Sit still.
SECOND SAILOR. Be sick, Mrs. . . *(Pause)*
GALACTIA. Why do you drink so much? Is it because—everybody is half cut round here, is it because—
SECOND SAILOR. Not the drink . . . *(Pause)* The picture. *(Pause)* Is death like that? In battle, is it? *(Pause)*
GALACTIA. Yes. I have never seen it, but I think so.
SECOND SAILOR. I think so, too. *(Pause)*
GALACTIA. Sit there, and I'll draw you . . .
SKETCHBOOK. The Young Sailor Struck. *(Pause)* The Young Sailor Struck does not exist in any of the preliminary sketches for The Battle of Lepanto, and a close examination of the paint reveals him to be an addition to the composition added at a later stage. He is shown huddled against an abandoned cannon, staring with an expression of disbelief at the violence raging about him. It is the only face in the entire canvas of over two hundred faces which is in repose, and painted in a liquid, translucent colour in an almost religious manner, acts as a barometer of human incomprehension, in contrast to the fixed and callous stare of the Admiral Suffici against whom he is placed in diametrical opposition. The two figures are separated by a shoal of dying figures sliding out the canvas to the left, while to the right, in the third point of a triangular configuration, in utter desolation against the mayhem, The Man With The Crossbow Bolt In His Head covers his ears, rocking to and fro at his oar, fathoming the shock of what's befallen him and inviting us to share his passionate desire to be somewhere else . . .

Scene Nine

A passageway in the palace.

OFFICIAL. Signor Carpeta?
CARPETA. Yes.
OFFICIAL. Take a seat, please. Have you brought your folder?
CARPETA. Yes.
OFFICIAL. What a big folder!
CARPETA. Yes, I do a lot of art.
OFFICIAL. Wait here, please.
SORDO *(emerging)*. Carpeta! You here, too!
CARPETA. Naturally.
SORDO. Same old faces. Same old hacks!
CARPETA. I don't think you should call yourself a hack, or you will start

to believe it.

SORDO.   I do believe it! I am a hack. And so are you.

CARPETA.   I have no wish to be included in your—

SORDO.   You may not wish it, old son, but—

CARPETA.   I resent that, Sordo. No, more than that. It makes me angry. If you do not wish to paint seriously, you should not paint at all.

SORDO.   Excellent. What have you brought along, Christ Among The Flocks, is it? Oh, don't be angry, it's as much a performance as my self-denigration and twice as difficult to keep up. They are looking for movement.

CARPETA.   Movement?

SORDO.   Yes, it's a secular subject.

CARPETA.   What?

SORDO.   Ah, well, you wait and—

OFFICIAL.   Signor Carpeta!

SORDO.   We must get together, have a talk some time—

CARPETA.   Yes—

SORDO.   They call us a school of painters but we never meet, except at funerals. Funny school!

OFFICIAL.   Signor Carpeta!

Scene Ten

A room in the palace. The door closes.

OSTENSIBLE.   Thank you for your folder.

CARPETA.   Oh, I—

OSTENSIBLE.   It's too big.

CARPETA.   I'm sorry.

URGENTINO.   Really, we scarcely need educating in the nature of your talent, Signor Carpeta.

CARPETA.   Thank you.

URGENTINO.   Or perhaps you thought the Head of State has not the time to keep abreast of current movements in the field of painting? Christ Among The Flocks! There, you see!

CARPETA.   I am delighted you—

URGENTINO.   This is Cardinal Ostensible. He knows Christ Among the Flocks.

OSTENSIBLE.   I have one.

URGENTINO.   He has one! You see, you are among admirers here!

CARPETA.   I also have a number of secular drawings which you may—

URGENTINO. The Cardinale, as you know, is Secretary of State for Public Education, which is to say he is very worried about Signora Galactia and so am I. Sit down, will you? Let me tell you straight away that any time I spend on the subject of art is not wasted. Art is opinion, and opinion is the source of all authority. We have just spoken to Sordo. He is spent, don't you think? Quite spent?

CARPETA. He is only thirty-seven . . .

URGENTINO. What does it matter if he's seventeen? He's spent.

CARPETA. Perhaps.

OSTENSIBLE. They pretend to be kind to one another, but they are each other's cruellest critics. How well do you know Galactia?

CARPETA. I know her.

OSTENSIBLE. I didn't ask that, I said how well. Very well? Or hardly well?

CARPETA. Pretty well.

URGENTINO. They say you go to bed with her. Pretty often.

CARPETA. Do they?

OSTENSIBLE. They say so. Of course they may be wrong. And in any case to go to bed with someone is not to know them, I suspect. Were they to be known to one another, to go to bed would for most people, be something of a problem, I dare say. And, conversely, you might sleep with someone every night and after ten years turn around and say, in honesty, you knew them only 'pretty well'. I speculate.

CARPETA. I have had a relationship with Signora Galactia of a—of a rather casual nature which—which is rather casual . . .

OSTENSIBLE. Yes . . . Yes . . . *(Pause)*

URGENTINO. You see, I have the most profound respect for Signora Galactia, as a painter, as a woman.

CARPETA. Me, too. I think she—

URGENTINO. Don't interrupt—

CARPETA. I'm sorry—

URGENTINO. A profound respect. She is not spent. Most certainly she is not spent; she moves, she travels, a sort of meteor cleaving her way through dark spaces, undisturbed by gravities, I mean the gravities of greater stars, she is under no influence but her own will, she has by her perseverance—and possibly, perversity—achieved a following, she has a school of sorts, and she is brilliant. And the Cardinale and I thought, decided between ourselves, we could not let Venice fail to celebrate her genius, because for an art establishment like us, a cynical clique of bureaucrats like us, who like to pride ourselves on taste, to let a great fish through the net of our sponsorship would be a lapse. I tease you, but we hate to miss anyone.

OSTENSIBLE. We hate to miss you.

URGENTINO. We hate to miss you, too. And so we adopted her. Talent is rare and precious, and of course, explosive too. What is the matter with her, is she mad? *(Pause)*

CARPETA. Mad? Is she mad? She—yes, she may be a little mad, she—keeps asking me to leave my wife. And—so on. It is a sort of madness.

URGENTINO. Is it? I should have thought that rather depended on your wife. Or perhaps she loves you.

CARPETA. Loves me, well, she—

URGENTINO. Loves you. More than you are worth. I have seen the painting called The Battle Of Lepanto in various stages and it is not getting any better, it is getting worse, not from the technical point of view but from the moral one. And I ask you very frankly, is she a moral woman?

CARPETA. Moral? No, I don't think you could—not moral, no. *(Pause)*

OSTENSIBLE. How quickly can you paint a canvas of three thousand square feet, Signor Carpeta? *(Pause)*

CARPETA. A month.

URGENTINO. Now, that's silly—

CARPETA. No, I'm saying—

URGENTINO. I have heard of ambition, but that's—

OSTENSIBLE. Let him finish.

CARPETA. I'm saying I *could*, I *could* paint a canvas of that size in a month, only it wouldn't be—

URGENTINO. It damned well wouldn't, would it?

CARPETA. be very—very good—

URGENTINO. Quite. You are not a rash man, Signor Carpeta. I am glad to see.

CARPETA. For a decent composition and—with the right assistants, I think—seven weeks.

OSTENSIBLE. You see, Signora Galactia has not been altogether fair with us.

CARPETA. No, no, she hasn't been—

OSTENSIBLE. She has—

CARPETA. Gone her own way—

OSTENSIBLE. Gone her own way, yes! Which is all very well in certain circumstances, but in a public matter such as this—

CARPETA. You have to think of —*(Pause)*

OSTENSIBLE. What? *(Pause)* What do you have to think of?

CARPETA. What—the circumstances—require. *(Pause)*

URGENTINO. Well, that's it, then, isn't it? Can you start today?

CARPETA. Yes.

OSTENSIBLE. The way you do Christ—the nobility of Christ—transmit that feeling to the officers.

CARPETA. Yes . . .

OSTENSIBLE. The battle is not—unwholesome—it is, rather, the highest moment of self-sacrifice. It is as divine—in essence—as the crucifixion—

CARPETA. Yes . . .

OSTENSIBLE. And the soldiers are—not victims of a sacrifice but—a fraternity on Christian crusade, do you follow?

CARPETA. Yes. But you must paint it for yourself! It is your painting!

OSTENSIBLE. It is his painting, yes!

URGENTINO. Congratulations! You are—from this moment, promoted to the pantheon of Venetian masters, yes, you are!

CARPETA. Thank you, it will be my finest opportunity to—

URGENTINO. Sordid financial matters can be arranged by others at a later date!

CARPETA. Of course, I long to satisfy both my own requirements as a painter and—

URGENTINO. Good bye! Good bye!

CARPETA. Thank you for—

URGENTINO. Do leave your folder. Yes, leave it. *(Pause. A door is closed)* Why is it, I wonder, the base instinct is so often the spur to fine achievement? I suspect Signor Carpeta will, in seven weeks, do his greatest for us, though it will be modest enough as greatness goes . . . Do you want any of his drawings? *(Turned cartridge paper)* There, that's quite good . . . and look! I swear that's Galactia naked . . .!

OSTENSIBLE. What about Galactia?

URGENTINO. She loves him . . . the great woman . . . dotes on . . . the little man . . .

OSTENSIBLE. Please.

URGENTINO. What about her?

OSTENSIBLE. We cannot overlook the provocation. We cannot, can we, on delivery of this calculated and obscene affront to History, lie down, can we? Say many thanks and put it in the basement? It is all meat and chopped up genitalia, it is not a battle and she knows it. We cannot simply overlook.

URGENTINO. No.

OSTENSIBLE. And she wouldn't want us to.

URGENTINO. She would hate it.

OSTENSIBLE. We have to make an appropriate response. *(Pause)*

URGENTINO. Prison.

OSTENSIBLE. You think prison?

URGENTINO. I think prison is—a little prison, not too much—is what this desperate woman wants . . .

URGENTINO. Yes.

URGENTINO. Confirmation. Of our baseness. Is what she wants.

Scene Eleven

The barracks.

GALACTIA. It's done. *(Pause)*

CARPETA. Yes. *(Pause)*

GALACTIA. IT'S DONE. And you will be the first to see it. Do you know I have never shown a finished canvas to a man before, a man first, except my father, and he taught me? Do you know you are the first?

CARPETA. Yes.

GALACTIA. I do it because I love you. I love you, Carpeta.

CARPETA. Yes. *(Aside)* I believe there is nothing so exquisite, so refined in its cruelty, as to be the object of a passion which you no longer reciprocate . . .

GALACTIA. Kiss me . . .!

CARPETA *(aside)*. It is humiliating, not of the one who loves you, but of you yourself. Splashed with adoration, it burns your skin . . .

GALACTIA. Kiss me . . .

CARPETA *(aside)*. And your lips moan. Sin in it, ache in the eyes . . . *(To her)* Is it really finished? I don't feel worthy of—

GALACTIA. Don't be silly!

CARPETA. Actually don't feel I deserve—

GALACTIA. Don't be so—what's the matter with you? Don't deserve—what are you—

CARPETA. Just—the honour—

GALACTIA. Be quiet, you'll spoil it for me! Stand there. There. Now, I will open all the shutters, and you—keep your eyes shut. Wait! Don't move! *(The shutters are flung open along the length of the room)* Don't turn round! I feel utterly childish about this. I—I have never made a cult of this, of first showings but—flood in, daylight! Look, clear, liquid light and—*(The last one clatters open)* Now, wait. *(Pause)* Open your eyes. *(Pause)* What? *(Pause)* Carpeta? *(Pause)* What, are you—are you crying? You *are* crying! Oh, my dear, you're crying! Because it's good, is it? *(His sobs become audible)* Is it that good? Tell me! OH, GOD, IS IT SO GOOD YOU HAVE TO—*(He wails)* Oh, wonderful, great lover, shh! *(Sound of hammering wood)*

Scene Twelve

Some hours later. The studio is dismantled.

SUPPORTA. It is a great waterfall of flesh. It is the best thing you have ever done. But I don't think, forgive me, I want to be associated with you any more. Professionally, that is.

GALACTIA. I competely understand—

SUPPORTA. No, let me finish, mother, please—

GALACTIA. Absolutely get what you—

SUPPORTA. YOU NEVER LET ME FINISH. *(Pause)* Because whilst it is your best work, I don't feel sympathy with what you—

GALACTIA. Quite! I am not in the least wounded by your rejection of me which—

SUPPORTA. Why do you—

GALACTIA. Which I thoroughly anticipated and therefore—

SUPPORTA. WHY WON'T YOU BE HURT! Always, you pretend to be prepared! I am giving up a professional relationship of twenty years, why don't you be hurt for just a minute? **(***Pause***)**

GALACTIA. Because it was obvious you would desert me, it was as clear as daylight to me I could not count on you any more.

SUPPORTA. I think you enjoy seeing people fail.

GALACTIA. Yes, I think I do. I expect it. I drive for it. And when it happens, all right, I'm gratified. I have shattered tolerance. You are a drapery painter, Supporta, you could not understand where I was headed and now you want—absolutely comprehensible!—to save yourself. Change your name or something. I don't care for your method anyway. Everything shines. Not all fabric shines, you paint too many highlights—

SUPPORTA. I think you are—I hate to say this—you are a little mad.

GALACTIA. Well, yes of course, you would reiterate the popular opinion. I must help them, they are taking it off the stretcher, I have to supervise them or they—

SUPPORTA. I am not deserting you, I am saying—

GALACTIA. *(to Workmen).* WAIT FOR ME, THERE! Listen, I am not injured. Set up a little studio, paint wedding pictures—

SUPPORTA. You always have to ridicule—

GALACTIA. Yes, dash it down! I haven't time to listen to your motives, and who cares about them anyway? If we all had to understand one another's motives! Christ! I will write you a cheque for your services—*(To Workmen)* DON'T DO THAT, THERE, IT'S NOT A CARPET! *(To SUPPORTA)* They are putting it on a barge, and the barge will sail up the canal, like some great bomb snuggled under tarpaulins, and they will unload it and carry it into the palaces of power, and it will tear their minds apart and explode the wind in their deep cavities, and I shall be punished for screaming truth where truth is not allowed. IT MADE CARPETA WEEP WITH ITS POWER!

Scene Thirteen

A room in the palace.

URGENTINO. It is hanging. It is not framed, but it is hanging. In the gallery.

SUFFICI. Let me see it.

URGENTINO. No hurry! No hurry! Finish your drink. *(Pause)* Finish your drink. *(Pause)* There comes a point—with painting—at which no amount of intervention can significantly alter the outcome of the project.

SUFFICI. It is not what you—

URGENTINO. It is not what Venice—*(Pause)*

SUFFICI. Ah. *(Pause)*

URGENTINO. Because of what I can only describe as a—mental disorder—which prevents the artist satisfying the aspirations of her customer. *(Pause)*

SUFFICI. It's—

URGENTINO. It's a bit—it's not like anything I've seen before. Or want to see again for that matter.

SUFFICI. I see. And I—I am—

URGENTINO. In it. Yes. You are. You figure very prominently, but—

SUFFICI. I want to see.

URGENTINO.   No hurry—

SUFFICI.   I want to see. *(Pause)*

URGENTINO.   Very well. It is an area of human activity in which control comes from within, in which the artist either exercises discretion, and wills discretion, or—I have got someone else doing one so it doesn't really matter what kind of mess she's made of—there. Feel free to be sick. *(Pause)* Spew up if you—

SUFFICI.   SHUT UP. *(Pause)* The hands—the hands are utterly vile. They are not my hands.

URGENTINO.   Nope.

SUFFICI.   Look, look at my hands, look at them—

URGENTINO.   Yes—

SUFFICI.   LOOK AT THEM!

URGENTINO.   I AM LOOKING AT THEM!

SUFFICI.   That is not a likeness of my hands, is it?

URGENTINO.   Of course it isn't—

SUFFICI.   My hands which are beautiful in fact, despite my age, are beautiful and not claws as she has painted!

URGENTINO.   Cesare—

SUFFICI.   Not claws, are they!

URGENTINO.   Cesare, you will have the servants running in—

SUFFICI.   What is the point of making me attend three sittings if she goes away and copies some talons out of—

URGENTINO.   Cesare—

SUFFICI.   some ornithological atlas!

URGENTINO.   I have never seen you so animated—

SUFFICI.   I am animated, I am animated!

URGENTINO.   Quite rightly, but—

SUFFICI.   Not because I am vain, I am the least vain of men, but because it is simply untrue—

URGENTINO.   Untrue, yes—

SUFFICI.   And consequently it is a lie, and I—

URGENTINO.   Abhor a lie, I know you do—

SUFFICI.   And the face—

URGENTINO.   The face is worse—

SUFFICI.   Whilst it looks like me—

URGENTINO.   Vague resemblance—very vague resemblance—

SUFFICI.   Is painted with contempt—

URGENTINO.   Well, we don't know—

SUFFICI.   It is contempt and you only have to see Garacci's portrait of me in the flower garden to see—

URGENTINO.   This is a different genre, but yes—

SUFFICI.   I am saying Garnacci understood me and this is—I am sorry to be so angry but—

URGENTINO.   No, no—

SUFFICI.   I am not normally angry but she simply cannot paint, she cannot be allowed to do this thing which is—in effect—a calculated offence to me and to the sailors who so heroically laid down their—what is this, what are all these bodies doing—it is all bodies, everywhere with gaping—I do not pretend to be an artist but it was not like that and my face is so contemptible!

Scene Fourteen

A room.

URGENTINO.   How are you feeling? *(Pause)* Are you feeling uncomfortable?

GALACTIA.   Yes. *(Pause)* And good at the same time.

URGENTINO.   How's that?

GALACTIA.   Virtuous. And scared.

URGENTINO.   Delicious combination. *(Pause)*

GALACTIA.   Firstly, I am—

URGENTINO.   Shut up—

GALACTIA.   I am prepared to repay every penny of the fee I—

URGENTINO.   Shut up. I have seen a drawing of your breasts.

GALACTIA.   What has that got to—

URGENTINO.   Shut up.

GALACTIA.   I don't see what that—

URGENTINO.   SHUT UP! *(Pause)* This is my palace. This is my cushion. You have your empire, I have mine. I said I have seen a drawing of your breasts. It is on my desk, look. WHAT AM I GOING TO DO WITH THAT PAINTING? *(Pause)* You should not think, because we are not artists, we are stupid. Because we are governors, or bureaucrats, stupid. Terrible error. Terrible vanity. Leads to the noose, the wall, the death chamber—

GALACTIA.   I take full responsibility for—

URGENTINO.   I DON'T CARE IF YOU TAKE RESPONSIBILITY OR NOT. *(Pause)* What do you think that means? 'I take full responsibility—'? Arrogant! Sit there, on my cushion, on the armorial of Venice, in your steam of cleverness, unafraid long jutting woman's jaw, HATE THAT! Really, humility would do you good. Please don't stare at me, look at the floor or something, what did you think you were doing, because the Committee is assembling and they are insulted, the republic is insulted, don't you like the republic? If you do not like it it is treason, don't tell me you didn't think of that?

GALACTIA.   Not terribly.

URGENTINO.   Not terribly, didn't terribly think of it, what are you—

GALACTIA.   CRY OF THE BLOOD. *(Pause)*

URGENTINO.   There is a bridge over there. On one side of the bridge there is a carpet. And on the other side of the bridge there is bare stone. And on this side of the bridge there are cushions, and on the other side there is straw. And on this side there are windows, but on the other side it is dark.

On this side we laugh, and on that side they cry. Do you know the bridge? *(Murmurs of approaching voices)*

GALACTIA. The Bridge of Sighs.

URGENTINO. Yes. I cannot tell you how it excites me to think of your bare breasts against the wall, and my buttocks on this brocade . . . *(The committee enter the room)*

GALACTIA. I am great. I am great because I conceded nothing, but utterly was myself. And all these artists hanging on the walls, were not themselves, but other people . . .

OFFICIAL. Sit down, please.

GALACTIA. I am prepared to refund to the State of Venice all monies I received for—

OFFICIAL. Silence, please, and sit down.

GALACTIA. I want to make this statement—

OSTENSIBLE. We do not want your statement—

GALACTIA. Why can't I make a statement?

OFFICIAL. Are you Anna Galactia, of Via—

GALACTIA. You know bloody well I am Galactia, everybody knows I'm Galactia, why else would I be here—

OFFICIAL. And are you the executor of the subject painting 'The Battle of Lepanto' which is hanging on the wall opposite the window there—

GALACTIA. Really, this is—what is the point of—

OSTENSIBLE. I think, ditch all that. Thank you. *(Pause)* Signora, we do not understand your painting.

GALACTIA. It is a painting of a battle at sea.

OSTENSIBLE. It is a slaughter at sea.

GALACTIA. A battle is a slaughter.

OSTENSIBLE. No, it is the furtherance of political ends by violent means.

GALACTIA. I showed the violence.

OSTENSIBLE. But not the ends. So it is untruthful. The ends were the freedom of the seas, the affirmation of the Christian faith, the upholding of a principle. Why did you not paint those?

GALACTIA. How do you paint the upholding of a principle?

OSTENSIBLE. You show it by the nobility of the participants.

PASTACCIO. Do you believe in the principle, Signora? *(Pause)*

GALACTIA. I am a painter, I'm not—

OSTENSIBLE. Oh, now, you cannot hide behind your sensuality, your instinct—

GALACTIA. Why not?

OSTENSIBLE. That is dishonest, that is trying to slam the gate on our debate, isn't it?

GALACTIA. I painted death because all I saw was death.

PASTACCIO. So you admit to being partial? You admit to attending to one aspect of the truth?

GALACTIA. Yes. And I don't admit it, I embrace it.

PASTACCIO. You admit to attending to one aspect of the truth to the exclusion of the other?

GALACTIA. What other?

PASTACCIO. The nobility of the struggle.

GALACTIA.   I deny its nobility.

OSTENSIBLE.   You deny the virtue of the actions of the State of Venice?

GALACTIA.   I—I suppose if you—

OSTENSIBLE.   You obviously deny it. And the evidence is in the portrait of the Admiral, who is presented with an expression of the utmost callousness—

GALACTIA.   Callousness?

OSTENSIBLE.   Well, what else is it?

GALACTIA.   I hadn't put a name to it.

OSTENSIBLE.   I will do it for you. It is callousness.

PASTACCIO.   You see, we have to get behind the picture, and you want us to look at the surface. You say, look at the surface, the brush strokes, the colour, the anatomy! Yes, all very good, that is your strength, who can quarrel with you on that territory? You are supreme. But behind the painting we are all equals. What are you saying? It seems to us you are saying you revile the State of Venice. Do you want to argue with that?

OSTENSIBLE.   Argue if you want. *(Pause)*

GALACTIA.   What are you going to do with me?

PASTACCIO.   Please, argue the point.

GALACTIA.   No.

PASTACCIO.   Why not?

GALACTIA.   Because you will only win the argument.

PASTACCIO.   How do we know until you have offered your defence?

GALACTIA.   No. I am not going to give you the satisfaction of proving me wrong. If the surface of the painting is my territory, the back of it is yours. You are specialists in arguments. I hate arguments. What are you going to do with me?

OSTENSIBLE.   I have never heard of an artist who did not want to engage with his opponents, there is nothing they love more than expostulating about their genius, what is the matter with you? Defend yourself or we shall become irritated.

GALACTIA.   You see, you must win.

OSTENSIBLE.   It is not a question of—

GALACTIA.   WIN. WIN.

OSTENSIBLE *(bitterly)*. NOT A QUESTION OF WINNING BUT OF—

GALACTIA.   Hang the painting. Take it in the street, and hang it.

OSTENSIBLE.   Never.

GALACTIA.   Why?

OSTENSIBLE.   Because there is the little matter of public morals, miss!

PASTACCIO.   Hang it in the street . . .!

OSTENSIBLE.   The artist's cry! The whine of the corrupter!

GALACTIA.   Ah, real thing now, the real strangler!

OSTENSIBLE.   The irresponsibility of your manner is of course, only a mask, the posture of artistic freedom, look at the way you dress, you have not washed that garment in God knows how many—

GALACTIA *(disbelief)*. How do you know when—

OSTENSIBLE.   And your breasts quite clearly unsupported—

GALACTIA.   How does he—

OSTENSIBLE. All calculated to make us think ARTISTIC IRRES-
PONSIBILITY, WELL, NO, WE ARE NOT FOOLED! *(Pause)* You are
an enemy of the Republic. You wish to destroy its unity and its power for
an end you will no doubt admit in time but the great thing is WE ARE
NOT FOOLED. *(Pause)* I really do despise artists and that is why I am so
perfectly qualified to sit on this committee. I despise artists as much as I
love art, and I can look at that plane before me, glistening with colour and
say it is an evil surface. There!
GALACTIA. I shall have to be punished, shan't I? You can't let someone
say—on the back of the canvas—all your principle is actually dirt, and
stench, and matted buttocks floating in the sea. I shall have to be broken in
some way. *(Pause)* Well, won't I? *(A door slams in a prison)*

Scene Fifteen

The prison.

GALACTIA. There's no light in here! Give us a candle!
GAOLER *(Receding).* No candles.
GALACTIA. No candles, no, of course not! A candle? What? Give you a
bit of light, give a painter colour? Don't be charitable.
MAN IN THE NEXT CELL. SHUT UP.
GALACTIA. Shut up, he says. Voice from the depths. Shut up. IT
STINKS IN HERE. I do think you might change the straw, the previous
occupant had crabs—no I haven't seen them, I speculate—
MAN IN THE NEXT CELL. SHUT UP.
GALACTIA. Shut up yourself! Get another room if you don't like it! It's
not as dark in here as you might think. Now, that is interesting. It's like
black, the colour black. People think there is only one black, but there is
black and black, there is black the absence of light and black—are we
under the canal here? UGH, I TOUCHED SOMETHING! *(She gasps
with horror)* I touched something, Oh, God, I . . .
MAN IN THE NEXT CELL. You have only been in there two minutes.
GALACTIA. Shut up, voice from the depths.
MAN IN THE NEXT CELL. TWO MINUTES.
GALACTIA. Well, of course it's difficult, I expected it to be difficult. I am
not surprised there is something disgusting on the floor, there would be
and I—UGH—*(The* MAN IN THE NEXT CELL *laughs)* Listen, my
friend, you have the advantage of experience, you mustn't take such
delight in—*(He laughs on)* All right, laugh on, laugh on, I never expected
to get an intellectual as a neighbour—
MAN IN THE NEXT CELL. WHO SAYS I'M NOT AN INTELLEC-
TUAL? WHO SAYS I'M NOT?
GALACTIA. Look at my squalor, look at my filth, this is what happens to
the one who loves the truth, I fully expected this, I was prepared for it, no

one visits me and when they do they tell me lies, NO WONDER. How long have I been here, you cannot count in the dark, the only proof that you have told the truth in this life is that you are punished for it! Am I to be tortured? I must be tortured, obviously, it would be inconsistent if I weren't tortured, driven mad and murdered in some corner. They hate the truth, don't they, they yank the teeth out of its mouth and kick the lips to blubber UNDERSTANDABLY IT'S A DANGEROUS THING. I shall say to the one who tortures me I FULLY UNDERSTAND YOUR MOTIVES, IT HURTS YOU, DOESN'T IT? I shall say that, which of course, only provokes more punishment, if you scream here can the Doge hear you? What sort of face have you got? You sound like you have a big nose.

MAN IN THE NEXT CELL. I have a big nose.

GALACTIA. Fancy that!

MAN IN THE NEXT CELL. I haven't seen my face for seven years.

GALACTIA. Well, we don't get mirrors, do we, we might grow vain, threading filthy straw through plaited hair and using shit for powder, mind you I was an untidy bitch to start with, paint up my fingernails and so on, though sometimes I liked to show off a bit, clean skirts and blouses, rather fragrant, but then I always forgot something, hair washing or turned up with dirty feet, I miss my lover, you lose your lover, don't you, lose your children, CALCULATED FACTOR IN THE PUNISHMENT, have an awful need of something physical and gross and old, banal thing up against the—WILL SOMEONE PUT A LIGHT ON . . .! *(Pause. Breathless)*

MAN IN THE NEXT CELL. Be still, because you have such a long time to endure. Be still, and preserve yourself. *(Pause)*

GALACTIA. Yes . . .

MAN IN THE NEXT CELL. Because if you scream and struggle you will wear down what you have, which is little enough in this bitterness. Be an animal in the straw. Be the toad.

GALACTIA. Yes . . .

MAN IN THE NEXT CELL. And slow your heart beat down.

GALACTIA. Yes . . .

MAN IN THE NEXT CELL. Lie, waiting. Hibernate the long winter of your offence.

GALACTIA. Thank you, yes . . .

MAN IN THE NEXT CELL. Anger, hang it up now. Prisons are such loud places. But only the quiet ones live. The noisy ones, they've carried passed my door . . .

Scene Sixteen

A studio in Venice.

URGENTINO. Ostensible wants to charge her with being an agent of the Sultanate. He likes to win an argument and she refused to argue with him, so now he's furious and says she is a Muslim. She is not a Muslim, is she? The exaggerated sense of mission is something I cannot stomach in clergymen. Since she is quite obviously not an agent of anyone except herself it will involve torturing her to a confession. I do think that is vile. Torturing and bribing witnesses. It is all extremely ghastly and has a lot to do with the fact of celibacy. Torture! Really, what are you to do with them? I would like more red there, where the sun is setting ... yes ... there ... perhaps orange, you say.

CARPETA. Orange.

URGENTINO. All right, orange. And she is in any case mad, I abhor a cliche, but you know it better than anyone. That figure is not very celebratory, I think—

CARPETA. This one—

URGENTINO. Holding the banner, yes, is not elated, is he?

CARPETA. He has got an arrow in his—

URGENTINO. Yes, but he is the standard bearer, isn't he, and standard bearers have to be elated because—that is why they are standard bearers, surely? There is altogether, and I'm sorry if I sound irritable, a certain lack of celebration in your work—

CARPETA. I have done everything you—

URGENTINO. Everything, I know, you have, you have—

CARPETA. Painting so quickly that—

URGENTINO. You have been wonderful, you have, and of course it is hurried in some respects—the horn blowers look a little—do you know Raphael?

CARPETA. Of course I know Raphael—

URGENTINO. Yes, well, he would have—

CARPETA. I'm sorry, I can't go on with this.

URGENTINO. More energy and—WHAT! *(Pause)*

CARPETA. I can't go on with this. *(Pause)*

URGENTINO. You're being silly.

CARPETA. I—

URGENTINO. Yes, you are, now, listen—

CARPETA. Endless interruption and—

URGENTINO. Shh, shh!

CARPETA. CAN'T GO ON WITH IT. *(Pause)*

URGENTINO. You are overwrought. The responsibility of accepting a commission of this scale is obviously—

CARPETA. It's not that—

URGENTINO. Yes, it is that and—

CARPETA. I WANT TO SEE GALACTIA. *(Pause)*

URGENTINO. Galactia? Why?

CARPETA. Because I love her and—

URGENTINO. You—

CARPETA. HAVE TO SEE HER. *(Pause)*

URGENTINO. I have taken a great risk in commissioning you to do this work—

CARPETA. I know and I—

URGENTINO. I took a great risk in commissioning her and I took a great risk in commissioning you and I—

CARPETA. I am sorry, I—

URGENTINO. I AM SICK OF BEING MESSED ABOUT BY ARTISTS. *(Pause)* You did not say you were in love with her, you said—

CARPETA. I know, I—

URGENTINO. Said it was a little—

CARPETA. I know I did—

URGENTINO. A sordid little sexual transaction.

CARPETA. I wanted to—

URGENTINO. WELL, NO YOU CAN'T, NOT UNTIL YOU'VE FINISHED IT, you—*(He gropes blindly)* It's not in my hands, it's the Committee of Public Education you should make petition to, not me—

CARPETA. You're the Doge—

URGENTINO. I am the Doge, but—

CARPETA. So you can—

URGENTINO. THIS IS A DEMOCRATIC COUNTRY!

RIVERA *(entering)*. Hello?

URGENTINO. I HATE YOU ALL.

RIVERA. What are you—

URGENTINO. I wish I had never seen a painting in my life! I blame you for this!

RIVERA. Me?

URGENTINO. Yes, you! You encouraged me, Rivera! I have been— through my own sensitivity—been drawn into needless conflicts with people who, crazed by self-indulgence, will not, and perhaps, God help them, cannot, sympathize with the problems of governing a modern state! Whereas I am forever having to sympathize with them, they are in love, they have a mission, they have a headache, they are menstruating. IT IS A MOST UNEQUAL RELATIONSHIP. *(Pause)* I sometimes wish I was a brute.

RIVERA. No, no . . .

URGENTINO. Yes, a brute with brute senses. Sending regiments to toss pianos out of windows. Really. You cannot imagine how I long to send pianos flying out of windows! But I don't, do I? I don't, and I am made miserable. *(He turns on* CARPETA*)* If you do not finish the painting, I will put you in a cell with her, there! And you can deliver babies on the filthy straw! *(He turns to* GINA*)* Gina, Gina, come here, come here! *(They walk away)* I am so upset, I cannot tell you. I am reduced to making threats against my favourite people, artists! Help me, tell me they are vaguely human, I am beginning to doubt my own perceptions . . . *(Whispers)* What is this painting like? The thing he's . . . tell me, is it—

RIVERA. Yes.

URGENTINO. What?

RIVERA. Shit.

URGENTINO. Is it? It is, isn't it! It is! I knew it was! Oh, God!

RIVERA. Sit down.

URGENTINO. Take me out of here—take me out—the smell of paint—I used to love a studio and now I could bring up my breakfast—he is a banal and gutless hack—

RIVERA.   That is not fair—

URGENTINO.   He is, he will not listen when I—

RIVERA.   He has listened, he has listened too much—

URGENTINO.   He has no imagination of his own, what do you expect me to do?

RIVERA.   He is a very sound painter of religious subjects, he is not an epic painter—

URGENTINO.   Why did he turn up, then? Imposter!

RIVERA.   It is an offence against art to flatter minor artists with projects they are not equipped to handle—

URGENTINO.   What am I do do, then!

RIVERA.   Will you be quiet for a moment?

URGENTINO.   I can't be quiet, I'm furious! *(Pause)* All right, what?

RIVERA.   I have seen Galactia's painting.

URGENTINO.   Ostensible wants it burned!

RIVERA.   Yes, but he won't. He will put it in a cellar. Now, listen to me, and I will tell you what I know, as a critic, and a loyal supporter of your party and your cause. In art nothing is what it seems to be, but everything can be claimed. The painting is not independent, even if the artist is. The picture is retrievable, even when the painter is lost . . .

Scene Seventeen

The prison. A door crashes back on its hinges. Pause.

CARPETA.   Galactia . . . Galactia? *(Sound of scraping on stone)* IS THERE A LIGHT IN HERE? *(Movement)* Are you there? It's me, are you there or—

GALACTIA.   Have you ever painted blind? *(She stops scraping)* Actually it isn't dark. We make so much of light, but light's relative. I now think daylight is terribly CRUDE.

CARPETA.   Where are you, I—

GALACTIA.   Clumsy thing you are, blundering in this little space. You can always find me by my smell.

CARPETA.   I—I—

GALACTIA.   It is a little fruity, isn't it? Like the badger's den and me the female badger, don't be frightened, look, I have drawn a man, in granite, with granite. It's you. In monochrome, but in this light who wants polychrome, or poly anything? Nothing's poly in a prison, it's all mono, mono dinner, mono supper, mono stench. This wall is covered with remarks, I could not read them for the first three months but—

CARPETA.   Three months? You have not been here three—

GALACTIA.   then you find them, treasures! Whole biographies, and sexual miseries, and me the first to make a picture! An artist always will, won't she, get decorating the cruel old wall of torture—

CARPETA. Listen, the Doge—

GALACTIA. The Doge? Kind Doge!

CARPETA. Has given me the letter of—

GALACTIA. Sweet, fat Doge! Listen—

CARPETA. No, you listen—

GALACTIA. YOU LISTEN TO ME. *(She whispers, urgently)* I find I am still fertile. I find, in this damp den, fertility back at my age! Lovely shock! Have you two minutes?

CARPETA. You aren't listening to me—

GALACTIA. I want a child, they are not allowed to execute the pregnant, I bleed again, you see, in this dank stillness, here, come here—

CARPETA. Look, I—

GALACTIA. Come, quick before they—

CARPETA. It isn't—I don't—

GALACTIA *(sarcastic)*. Oh, wonderful! Oh, reluctant Carpeta who was all over me once!

CARPETA. I can't actually see you and anyway—

GALACTIA. What does that matter? I want to lie in the straw like a badger, littering, quick do your stuff—

GALACTIA. NO.

GALACTIA. Why are you here? Don't smile, why are you here? Have they burned the Battle?

CARPETA. No.

GALACTIA. LIAR! Of course they have burned it and you have brought the ashes—

CARPETA. It is not burned—

GALACTIA. Of course it is burned, how could they tolerate it, it is too powerful for them, and I am too powerful for them, I am Galactia who told the truth and all you do is lie to me!

GAOLER *(entering)*. On yer way.

GALACTIA. Why do they lie to me? I tell you this, you with the bent back and the club fist, I like you best, you are no liar!

GAOLER. On yer way, I said. *(Pause)*

GALACTIA. What? *(Pause)* Don't smile at him. What is this?

GAOLER. Out. *(Pause)*

GALACTIA. Out? I live here.

GAOLER. Two minutes to get yer things—

GALACTIA. WHAT IS THIS? ALL THE TRUTH TELLERS LIVE HERE.

CARPETA. You're free. This is the order, look—

GALACTIA *(snatches it)*. Show me—

CARPETA. Signed by the—

GALACTIA. CAN'T SEE—IN THIS LIGHT, CAN'T—*(She screws it up)* I CANNOT BE RELEASED! HOW CAN THEY RELEASE ME I AM TOO DANGEROUS!

MAN IN THE NEXT CELL. Would you show a little slivver of consideration to the—

GALACTIA. THEY ARE RELEASING ME . . . !

MAN IN THE NEXT CELL.   Forgive me, I cannot work up any happiness
for you, but I have been here seven years, and it hurts me when someone
goes out, it hurts me terribly, so please enjoy your freedom quietly.
GALACTIA *(Quietly).* What did you do, strange dark thing in the straw?
MAN IN THE NEXT CELL.   Nothing. I did nothing. And that is why I
shall never be released. *(Pause)*
GALACTIA.   I'll paint you! I'll paint you and I will show your innocence!
MAN IN THE NEXT CELL.   Please, you—
GALACTIA.   TRUTH OF THE IMPERIAL JURISDICTION!
MAN IN THE NEXT CELL.   Please—
GALACTIA.   EXPOSE THE TRUTH AND BACK I'LL COME!
GAOLER.   Come on, you daft bitch—
GALACTIA.   Don't clean it out, I'm coming back! *(Suddenly she sobs,
falters)* Hold me, hold me oh, daylight . . .!

Scene Eighteen

*A public place. Subdued murmurs of a crowd passing in line before a
National Treasure.*

URGENTINO.   To have lost such a canvas would have been an offence
against the artistic primacy of Venice. To have said this work could not be
absorbed by the spirit of the Republic would be to belittle the Republic,
and our barbarian neighbours would have jeered at us. So we absorb all,
and in absorbing it we show our greater majesty. It offends today, but we
look harder and we know, it will not offend tomorrow. We force the
canvas and the stretcher down the gagging throat, and coughing a little,
and spluttering a little, we find, on digestion, it nourishes us! There will be
no art outside. Only art inside.
OSTENSIBLE.   THE MESSAGE. What about the MESSAGE.
URGENTINO.   Cardinal, your single-mindedness is a credit to your jesuit
professors, but you must stop hacking. The blunt, dull hack of Christian
persecution, the urge to the bonfire. Hate it. With all respect, hate it . . .
(Murmurs of crowd)
PRODO.   Thank you, thank you! That's me, I am the figure, thank you,
same bolt, same head! Note the bolt which I endured for my nation, this is
me here, a very reasonable likeness, I think you will agree, thank you, you
see I shudder in an ecstasy of patriotic fervour . . .!
SORDO.   It is a success.
LASAGNA.   You mean it is popular. Yes, it is popular . . .
SORDO.·   I mean, people like it.
LASAGNA.   Yes.
SORDO.   They have nicknamed it THE SLAG'S REVENGE. Galactia
has never kept a man. Several of the corpses look like Carpeta.

LASAGNA. And that's you, surely? With the javelin in the throat . . .

SORDO. And Bertocci, falling out of the rigging, yes!

LASAGNA. If it had been painted by a man it would have been an indictment of the war, but as it is, painted by the most promiscuous female within a hundred miles of the Lagoon, I think we are entitled to a different speculation.

SORDO. It is very aggressive. You and I, we wouldn't have been so aggressive. A woman painter has a particularly—female—aggressiveness, which is not, I think, the same as vigour. Do you agree with that distinction?

LASAGNA. Yes. It is coarse.

SORDO. Coarse, yes. Because she is so desperate to prove she is not feminine, a flower-painter, an embroiderer, she goes to the extremes and becomes, not virile, but shrill.

LASAGNA. It is shrill. It defeats its purpose by being shrill.

SORDO. She can paint, of course—

LASAGNA. She can paint, but it's excessive. And so is she.

SORDO *(pained)*. And yet they seem to like it . . .

LASAGNA. Carpeta! Giulio and I have been speculating as to whether that object there—that figure with the head slewed off—is actually you. The Slag's Revenge, you see. It has your teeth.

CARPETA. I don't think it matters what—

SORDO. Humour, Carpeta—

CARPETA. What you or any other—

SORDO. Oh, come on—

CARPETA. It is a public picture and you can't dishonour it! *(Pause)* Sorry. Just—the little nausea, you know, the little belch of loathing at the fellow artists gnawing at each other's bones. Passing disgust at sound of tooth on bone. Gone now. Gone now! *(Popular noise, then silence)*

Scene Nineteen

GALACTIA's *studio.*

RIVERA. May I come in?*(Pause)* May I, there is no light so I—*(She kicks something)* Ow!

GALACTIA. I don't have lights.

RIVERA. Could I just draw—

GALACTIA. Don't draw the curtains.

RIVERA. Well, where are you—

GALACTIA. In my black hole. In my gaol. *(Pause)*

RIVERA. I'm sorry if—

GALACTIA. Sorry? You PANDERED. You LIED. Got me out by LICKING AND LAPPING. One hundred feet of pain and you LICKED

IT SMOOTH.

RIVERA.   They had no intention of leaving you in gaol, it was a gesture and—

GALACTIA.   SMOTHERED MY DANGER. SHAMELESS CONCILIATOR. *(Pause)* There are some words, in this mendacious time, this age of mendacity, which still bear filth and evil and the worst of those is CONCILIATOR! Unclean word!

RIVERA.   I promise you a week was all they intended to—

GALACTIA.   CONCILIATOR! *(Pause)*

RIVERA.   Yes . . . *(Pause)* You are terribly difficult to deal with. I thought—I honestly believed—you wanted the picture to be seen. I'm sorry. I really do not understand you—

GALACTIA.   I am not meant to be understood. Don't you see? Oh, you miserable, well-meaning, always-on-the-right-side, desperate little intellect! Death to be understood. Awful death . . .

RIVERA.   They are flocking to the exhibition. The hanging in San Marco. Doors are jammed and—

GALACTIA.   Any soldiers trampled on their tunics? Much mutiny down the docks?

RIVERA.   What?

GALACTIA.   I can't hear rioting, but the curtains are thick . . .

RIVERA.   In my catalogue I talk about the anatomy, which is—some people say they can touch the flesh, such is the realism of it, they—*(Pause)* Listen, it is art I am interested in. I have saved your art. Get up.

GALACTIA.   Carpeta came. Holding a little bag. My lover, left his wife—

RIVERA.   Get up, will you!

GALACTIA.   Little bag in the doorway, and I thought, I do not need you, it is so terrible to know I do not need you anymore . . .

Scene Twenty

The exhibition.

PRODO.   The figure on the right is me. Same bolt, same head, thank you, who got this disability in service of my nation, sweeping the atheistic power from the sea—

GALACTIA.   Doing all right, Prodo?

PRODO.   Signora Galac—

GALACTIA.   Shh!

PRODO *(quietly)*.   Signora, it has been a godsend, what with winter coming on—

GALACTIA.   Nothing's in vain! Nothing is wasted! If one beggar is kept from starving, no effort is too extreme! What do they say, you know more than any critic, what do they say? Trash, do they say?

PRODO.   Unfortunately I am obliged by the custodian to perch here at the right end of the picture, so they pass me as they enter, and they have no opinion. It is the other end, the exit, you should listen. One hundred feet later, a man might change his mind about many things. Some have catalogues, but most can't read. The ones who can't read gasp, the ones with catalogues go 'mmm'. So it's either gasp or mmm take yer pick. Excuse me, I must get on. *(He declaims)* This is me, my portrait at the moment of my agony, in service of my nation . . . (GALACTIA *passes along the murmuring crowd)*

GALACTIA. What do you think?

MAN. Me?

GALACTIA. Yes, what do you think of this? *(Pause)* Incredible or— *(Pause)* Or not? *(Pause)* Have you come far to—

MAN. The Piave—

GALACTIA. The Piave! You know I've never seen the Piave! To see a picture—that is rather a long way to see—I'm not trying to accost you, don't look for the custodian—I AM NOT ACCOSTING YOU—He thinks I—I just—*(Pause)* I painted it. It's mine. All right? I did the— *(Pause)* No, I'm not mad. Please don't look at me as if I'm mad—I STRENUOUSLY DENY THAT I AM MAD I JUST—*(Pause)* He's holding my hands . . . he's holding my hands . . .!

URGENTINO *(wading in)*. Galactia comes, not to admire her work—she is not so vain—but to admire the admirers! The queue is fifty metres long and the man there has returned eight times, ask him, it is a fact, he kneels there and he weeps. Look, you have drawn tears from him, wrung water from his coarse imagination! Do you feel powerful? I have such power, but no such power. I can make men weep, but only by torturing them, while you— don't resent me. In a hundred years no one will weep for your painting, only respect it. Cold, dull respect. Enjoy your peculiar authority! It is a great nation, is it not, that shows its victories not as parades of virility, but as terrible cost? My brother accepts he is a calculating man, but admirals must be! You have winkled out his truth, he is full of admiration for you, hands notwithstanding! Will you dine with us? I hate to miss a celebrity from my table. *(Pause)*

GALACTIA. Yes.